# HOMESTEAD
# BOY

# HOMESTEAD
# BOY
◆ ◆ ◆

*To Barbara,*
*Dr. Charles Beardsley*
*June 9-78*

True Tales of
the Old West
## CHARLES
## BEARDSLEY

introduction by
**Sally Hayton-Keeva**

Library of Congress Catalog Card Number 89-62661

ISBN 0-937959-88-x

Publishing consultant: Falcon Press Publishing Co., Inc.,
Helena and Billings, Montana.
Cover and book design by Steve Morehouse

To Sally Hayton-Keeva, who insisted I write this book. To Dr. Grant Venerable, who helped organize and publish the book. To all the loving friends, family, and teachers upon whose souls I have fed. And to my mother, Alice Broman Beardsley, who was my teacher in the classroom and in life and whose steady belief often kept me going.

# Contents

# Foreword

There is perhaps no time in history more romantic to the collective imagination than the years cowboys, gold prospectors, and pioneers settled in the untamed wilderness of the American West. Covered wagons and Indian campfires are still vivid images, as are those of the litle sod house, the dance hall girl, and the skull of a buffalo.

But what was it like to live in the West before it became memory; to live in a time when people kept lamps burning in their windows to help lost travelers find their way or rushed to help a neighbor catch a renegade bull or bear a child?

Through the clear eyes of a young boy, author Charles Beardsley recounts what it was like living in Ismay, Montana, in the years before the Great Depression, when houses were still lighted by kerosene lamps and the "bus" to the one-room schoolhouse was an old plowhorse. In a style reminiscent of a homespun *Canterbury Tales*, the author's prose verse is spare, charming, and as unassuming as the stories themselves.

Though now in his eighties, this poet, musician, and professor has lost none of the child's wonder and curiosity about the world around him. In vivid detail he recreates a way of life that is no more. Cowboys and preachers, prostitutes and mail order brides people the harsh Montana landscape. Quivers of Indian arrows are stil to be found where they were dropped in flight across the prairie, and signs of the passing of animals still recorded by ancient springs. Outhouses, Sears and Roebuck catalogues, and vile but effective home remedies all find their way onto the page, as they did into the life of the homestead boy.

Some events, like the death by drowning of a neighbor's child, are tragic. Others are frankly amusing, as in the story "Lillian and Rose."

> Rose was the oldest of eight girls.
> They were named after flowers.

When the last one came
my grandmother said they should have named her Cactus.
Maybe it would stop any more from coming.

Nothing escapes his vigilant eye; from a giggling girl's new dress to the number of holes in a rancher's outhouse. He writes:

A young boy sees things adult people cannot see
because adults are looking for specific things.
A young boy looks at everything.

It is fortunate that these stories have now been told, for the town and the prairie homesteads where they took place have sadly changed. When the author returned in later years, it was to find the bustling little town of Ismay nearly disappeared. Gone were the grain elevators, the drugstores, and the dentist. Gone the brothel and the schoolhouse. Most of the homesteaders, given so little land to build their dreams upon, had finally left the prairie for the city, defeated by drought and hunger and disappointment. Their small ranches had been swallowed by larger ones, and their homes left alone to brave the forces of nature.

There is no going home again for any of us. And yet, in these pages, those desperate, difficult, and—in spite of all, *happy*—years of settling that part of the West materialize before our eyes and we, too, bear witness to a time and a people gone forever.

SALLY HAYTON-KEEVA

# Preface

Dr. Charles Beardsley grew up in the world of the last pioneers. His parents (his mother, a school teacher, and his father, a newspaper man) followed one of the last pioneer movements, when the Chicago and Milwaukee Railroad opened up the land in eastern Montana to the homesteaders. This land had been the land of the Crow Indians, who were followed by a brief period of huge cattle ranches, and then came the arrival of the homesteaders. The government gave each applicant a half section of land if he would build a house, fence it in, and live in it for three years. It was a culture that lasted from 1910 to 1936 when the great dust bowl and Depression caused everyone to move away.

It is of this period that Dr. Beardsley writes. He writes neither poetry nor prose but tells true stories in the cadence and rhythm of the storyteller.

In *Homestead Boy*, Dr. Beardsley has tried to record some of the real life events that happened in this brief historical period. He does not moralize, and he allows the reader to establish his own moral interpretation. In one aspect, his stories are like ballads, and some have been set to music.

# Introduction

The settling of the Old West over a century ago may have contributed more than any other factor to America's status as a modern superpower. Stories left us by those rugged souls who inhabited this much-fabled era still grip the imagination—stories that became the stuff of which legends are made, not to mention made-for-Hollywood cinematic thrillers. For these were tales of adventure and romance; courageous settlers and mythical cowboys and Indians; and righteous lawmen who brought willful outlaws to swift and deserved justice.

But there is another side to the story, the story that really happened and the story seldom told because those who knew it have long vanished, along with the remarkable time that contained them. Which is why Charles Beardsley's book *Homestead Boy* is such an exciting addition to America's literature about itself. This heart-warming narrative recalls Beardsley's childhood in Montana in a bygone era, lost in a temporal "side street"of American history. This was no fictional "Twilight Zone," but truly an intense, if fleeting, pocket of time. Coexisting unseen, alongside a rapidly urbanizing world of electricity, refrigeration, automobiles, and indoor plumbing, the eastern Montana frontier period was both seductive and ennobling; licentious as well as Victorian. And it produced, in concentrated form, human experience of virtually every description. Cut off from the maddening pace of a twentieth century whose modern ways rarely intruded, the homestead period was in all respects a compressed, "final edition" of the Old West.

Begotten of a Chicago & Milwaukee Railroad and government land give-away and development scheme, this forgotten period (ca. 1910 to 1935) is set in the town of Ismay, where the author spent his boyhood. In a rich collection of essays, Beardsley depicts life as it was, when dreamers and homesteaders from the neighboring Midwest abandoned comfortable early twentieth-century conveniences to invade the former land of the Crow Indians and the prairie grass and the ghosts of once-great buffalo herds to eke out a living on reluctant soil.

*Homestead Boy* is important because it tells us about ourselves—who we were and what we have become. It provides us with a temporal link with our pioneering ancestors of the eighteenth and nineteenth centuries—those independent spirits who dared to hitch their wagons to their dreams, to breathe free in a westward "promised land."

A celebrated graduate of Eastern Montana College (1929), Beardsley attended eight other colleges and recently was awarded the degree of doctor of humanities. A renaissance man, Beardsley has spent his four-score plus years in far-ranging endeavors: from teacher in the fabled one-room schoolhouse to choral and band conductor, dramatist, "French Impressionist" painter, land developer, lay minister and Protestant theologian, college instructor, counselor, philosopher, and author. A recent president of the Sonoma Valley Historical Society, he has been a cultural mover and a dynamic force behind historic preservation. He makes his home in the wine country in the city of Sonoma, site of the 1846 Bear Flag Revolt and the first capital of California.

DR. GRANT VENERABLE

# The Buffalo Wallow

There were great, green circles on the virgin plain,
whenever a gentle summer shower came.
They were filled with bright, white mushrooms.
Mother would gather tubfuls
and we would feast on golden fried mushrooms
and rich, brown, homemade bread.

How were we to know that those bright, green circles
were the remnants of a forgotten Indian hunt,
where the Indians would gather up the buffalo skulls
and pray for the souls of those they slaughtered
and thank them for their gift of food and shelter.

There were few remnants of those great herds
that swept the untouched plains
enriching the soil as they feasted
on the rich prairie grass.
It was so tall that my homestead mother would worry
that her children would be lost in it.

The buffalo were the sustenance of the Indians,
bringing them food, shelter, tools, and clothing.
But the white man, covetous of the Indian land,
sent men to kill the sustenance of Indian lives.
By the thousands they killed them,
taking from them only their hides.
And their bodies lay stinking on the plains.

Down by the eastern gate of the barbed wire fence
was a dusty, dry hollow where these massive beasts
would dust themselves, wallowing in the sandy soil.
When the snows of winter melted,
the cool water made a pond.

My father had planted trees
to shield the northern side of the
lonesome homestead house.
Our trees were to die in those awful drought years.
But the seed of one of them
found its searching way
to grow beside the muddied pond.

Mother always loved all living plants.
She would gather ferns and flowering clematis
to plant them by her house and those
        of neighbors
to hide their barren lonesomeness.
The homestead people now are gone.
They could not eke out a living
on the sometimes barren homesteads.

Great machines now sweep over the land
with many noisy tractors planting wheat
        and then harvesting it.

But the buffalo wallow still remains.
A sometimes full, oft-times dusty hollow.
But the great green tree hangs over it.
The souls of the buffalo and the Indians,
who loved all living things,
hang over it in the great green tree.

*October 16, 1987*

The caterpillar tractor arrived just after the First World War. Only the rich could buy one. The small landowners, who farmed with horse-drawn vehicles, started to vanish.

# Myrtle and Roanie

When we settled on the rolling hills
of eastern Montana
there were no fences and few neighbors.
Dad built a tar paper house.
It looked like the drawing a child would draw.
A two-story with living room downstairs
and two shed rooms, one for a kitchen,
the other for a papa and mama's bedroom.
We three little children, and our fifteen-year-old
        half sister,
slept in a loft reached by ladder.
Sister Myrtle was everything to us.
She cared for us and kept old Frank
hobbled on the rich prairie grass,
changing his picket pin each day.
She learned to ride horse bareback
and leapt on him with a single jump.
Finally a cowboy gave her a saddle
and she learned to ride the toughest horse.
She had a riding skirt made
which was really two skirts, one for each leg.
There were few women but many cowboys,
and sometimes twenty cowboys would show up
to escort Myrtle to country dances many miles away.
Each hoped he would get the first or last dance
so that he could tell the world he was the best liked.
Shorty Lewis would play the fiddle and beat
        a bass drum with his foot,
while Mrs. Lewis chorded on the auto harp.
Myrtle would arrive home tired, sleepy, and happy.
The cowboy days were soon to end.
Within a short time the homesteaders
fenced up the homesteads with harsh barbed wire.
The big cattle owners still existed for a while.

School sections and railroad sections
were still unfenced.
In 1915 a horrible winter storm came.
Fences were covered deep in snow.
Herds of cattle and sheep froze to death.
In the spring, when we trudged over to see
        Grandmother,
we had to hold our noses because of the
        terrible smell.
One dead cow lay with her calf halfway out.
The cowboys left. One who had admired my sister most
sold his silver mounted saddle to get out of town,
but he gave Myrtle his most precious possession,
        his horse Roanie.
I don't think Roanie was very happy
with four little boys climbing all over him.
He always seemed to be dreaming
of the days when he chased wild cattle
        on the open prairie.

*August 1988*

# The Day I First Saw God

We spent our summer on the old homestead
where Mother, by being there,
could prove our rights to the homestead,
but the tarpaper house was too cold for winter
so we all returned to Sioux Falls,
riding for two days in the smoky day coach.
Dad always got free passes,
as he often worked on newspapers.
That winter we rented the Alrich house.
I was four and my favorite playmate
was the coal carrier's son who lived next door.
Mother was entertaining her Quilting Club
and she told brother John, age seven,
      to watch me.
He went to play with his best friend,
and I went to play with the coal carrier's son.
His father had come home for lunch
and left his loaded coal wagon in front of his house.
My little friend said, "Let's get on it."
He climbed up the spokes of the rear wheel,
but when I tried it, the horses reared
and the wagon wheel passed over me.
The coal carrier's wife was working upstairs.
She jumped out of the second story window
and grabbed me before the front wheels reached me.
She carried me, bleeding from the mouth,
to my crying mother, who called a doctor.
He examined me and said to my mother,
"There is no hope, he will not live."
My mother called another doctor.
He was called homeopathic.
He came in a black buggy with a white horse.
He had a long white beard that tickled me when
      he bent over.
His hands passed over me gently.

This photo was taken the year before "The Day I First Saw God."

He said to my mother, "He will live."
He gave me some medicine and came each day
and always laughed and told me stories.
    I knew he was God.
Several months later, when the ice man came by,
we always went out to get the slivers of ice
from the back end of his truck;
I was able to hobble along with them.

*August 1988*

# Flour Sacks

Flour was the principal food
the homesteaders bought.
They had cream, milk, meat, lard, and vegetables.
They prized the flour sacks, which became many things.
Pieced together they became tablecloths and sheets
and were often made into night clothes
and girls' underwear.
Floy Nolls' mother made her daughter
      a pair of bloomers.
When she climbed a ladder one day,
across her little bottom was the word "Climax."
The little boys sang
"I see London, I see France, I see somebody's
      underpants."

*September 1988*

# The Eastern Schoolteacher

There were few unmarried women in the old West.
The principal source for brides was the prostitutes
      of the red light district.
If a woman lived with a man for an unbroken year
she could claim herself married to him.
We always knew they were not common-law wives
if they went away for a month's vacation.
Lonely educated girls hoped to find
a husband in one of those isolated ranches.
One was hired to teach the school by the
      Powder River Bridge.
There was one hired to teach a little school
far up the Powder River, which used to be
called "a mile wide and an inch deep."
They had to cross the river on a cable.
As she swung on the long cable
she went into hysterics—she was sure she would drown.
She grabbed the cable and got a rope burn on her hands.
They reached the dance at the tiny schoolhouse.
The first cowboy that asked her to dance,
in his wild antics, he stepped on her ankle so badly
she fainted and fell limp on the floor.
They raised her up and put her head out the window
      to get more air to bring her to.
The window pane fell on her head
      and knocked her out.
The next stage carried her out of town.
She vowed she would seek romance closer to home.
There wasn't any in the West!

*September 1988*

Jesse Scott McCoy, county superintendent, visits the North Cottonwood School. At the time she had seventy schools to visit each year. Now there are only fifteen.

# How a Country Boy Learns about "The Thing"

Myrtle was to return home with her new baby.
She had gone to be with her natural mother
        when the baby came.
She was my half-sister—I wondered
        how a person could be a half.
But we loved her very much, she was so good
        and kind.
We had hurried home from school.
We climbed the cold attic stairs
to peep through a knothole as
we knew they would be coming through
the eastern gate and this was
the highest point to see them coming
        in their horse and buggy.

I asked my brother John where
        did she get a baby.
John said, "Don't you remember how fat
our mother got before
Edgar and Richard came?
Our father had planted a seed in her.
It grew and came out."
I had seen my mother planting seeds
        in the garden with a hoe.
 I said, "How did the seed get into her?"
He said, "Our father had a thing
between his legs just like the one you have."
He said, "Take down your pants."
I did, and saw that little thing
I used to play with when no one was looking.
I wondered how that little thing
that sometimes became stiff and hard
could ever plant a seed like a hoe.

The buggy arrived and Myrtle brought
        the new girl baby in.
I looked at her husband Phil, strong
and handsome, and wondered if his
seed planter was larger than mine.

I started to look at all the creatures
on the farm. It seems they were all planting seeds.
The rooster would run after the hens
and jump on them while the hens squawked loudly
        and acted like they enjoyed it.
I never saw a rooster's thing.
It was covered with feathers
and seemed to enter into the area where
her manure came out.

I watched the boar ride the sow
while she stood seeming happy.
The boar's thing was like a long corkscrew.
It seemed to turn around and around
as it entered just under the tail.
When her piglets came we had to sit in the barn
and watch her piglets being born.
She would try to eat them
and we would hit her on the nose to stop her.

We took old mare Betsy to the neighbor's stallion.
His thing was as long as your arm
and had a flat knob on the end.
He would make funny whinnying sounds
as he seemed to pump his seed in her.
We watched the bull mount the cow
when we brought the cows home from the pasture.
His thing was long, pink, and pointed.

Sometimes when the cowboys took away the two
        little balls below the thing,
they would take these balls and cook
them on the branding iron fire.
They called them mountain oysters,
        but I would not eat them.
When they had taken away these two balls,
the animal became very quiet and lovable.
They would sometimes try to ride a cow
        but no pink thing came out.

Sometimes a cow would have trouble with a seed.
The calf would not come out—
        only its legs came out.
Brother John tied a lariat to
        the calf's leg and, with
a rearing horse, pulled out the calf.

Sometimes someone had made a bad mistake.
Our neighbor had a horse with
his pink thing coming out under his tail,
and he would chase after a mare
with the long pink thing whipping behind
        him as he ran after the mare.
Another neighbor had a pink-white horse;
        they called him "Pinky."
He didn't seem to know what he was.
He didn't have a pink thing, nor did
        he have a bag between his legs like the males had,
but he would gather up all the mares and
        herd them together.
If a stallion tried to take one of them away,
small as he was, he would run up to them
        and kick them in the stomach and they
        would leave.

It seemed that everywhere seed was being planted
by everyone who came along.
I asked my mother why humans could
        only have one partner.
She said, "God said there should be only
        one woman for every one man."
I said, "Didn't Father hear him?"
I knew he had two children by another woman.
        She did not answer.

Our neighbor was a woman who had
        three children.
Her husband had run away and she married
        her hired man.
He always took the fifteen-year-old girl
        with him when he rode the range.
She was pretty, tall, and slightly cross-eyed.
She would help us learn to read and
        hold us on her lap in school.
She vanished and whispering neighbors
said the man had planted the seed in her
        and sent her away.
The sheriff found her and the man
was sent to prison, but his wife
got him out. She needed someone to run the farm.

My mother would have been surprised
if she had known what we heard from
        the hired man's talk
how on Saturday night they would
go to a place in town where
they could plant their seed.
The woman would receive many men
        just like the animals did.

And there was a very pretty girl,
but she was always naughty they said.
At a country picnic a gang of us
followed her and a country boy,
a handsome fellow, into the bushes
where we found him humping her
just like the animals did.
He had planted the seed in her.
It grew and her mother killed it with
        a hat pin and the girl died.

In later years I worked in a drug store.
I learned the sad story of young girls
who had the seed planted in them.
And they tried to kill it before it came out
and they died doing it.
No farmer plants a seed and then kills it.
Why does man kill his seed?
I was puzzled.

# Investigation

Our neighbors who had rented the Mason place
        had two daughters
who were very much fun to play with.
My brother Dick, who was three years younger,
said, "Let's play Mommy and Daddy today
and see how they make babies."
We showed the girls our little things
and the girls pulled up their skirts.
We rubbed our thing against theirs
        and nothing happened.
I thought this was a silly way to make babies.
I later learned how babies were made.
It wasn't as silly as I thought!

*August 1988*

# The Schoolmaster

I was seventeen when I went to the closest Teachers'
      College a hundred miles away.
I couldn't bear the harsh life, the cold winters and
      hot summers.
I had sixty dollars, a trunk of hand-me-down clothes,
and my precious books.
I got a job as houseboy, washing clothes and dishes,
shoveling snow, and caring for the house and yard.
My father had driven me there and helped me find a job.
He had no money to get home with
so I gave him half of mine—it left me with thirty dollars.
I was never hungry, but I didn't have any money
      to buy a pair of mittens,
so I tucked my hands inside the sleeves of my old coat.
Spring came, as it always does,
and the county superintendent of Custer County
asked me if I would like to teach the Five Mile School.
It was in the badlands area near Powder River.
The children had been so rebellious
that they had run off three teachers.
One had sued the school board
and had received a large settlement.
so there was little money left.
I might have to wait for my salary.
My brother John took me there.
The schoolhouse was made of cottonwood logs
      and the heavy winter snows
made it bulge out like a fat lady in a girdle.
It was held up by log braces.
Inside, the book shelves were an old mahogany bar
with marks of whiskey bottles on the shelves.
There was a huge coal stove in the middle of the room,
      rows of double seated desks,
a raised platform for the teacher,

with slabs of real black slate for a blackboard.
Mrs. Shook, who was the school secretary,
said I could board with them for thirty dollars a month.
Mr. and Mrs. Shook had a lean-to bedroom off the kitchen.
Mr. Shook's sister, whose husband had been sent to prison,
was there with two sons and two daughters,
        and his brother Will, who trained polo ponies,
        added to the household.
I had a room to myself, which they had carefully whitewashed.
My bed's legs stood in cans of kerosene
to keep the bed bugs out, but I could see them
        dancing on the ceiling
when I read my books by kerosene lamp
        that kept the ceiling warm.
Granny, who had come with them from the Caroline Mountains,
        and Mrs. Brown and the two girls
        slept in the living room.
Uncle Will and the two boys slept on a big bed
in the huge kitchen.
No one went to bed until I vacated the kitchen
so I went to bed early with my beloved books.
The house was made of nearly rotten cottonwood logs
and the roof was covered with red crushed rock
in which night-blooming cereus often filled the night
        with perfume.
The Shooks lived mostly off the land.
There were deer, antelope, and sage hens to kill,
and they had cows and chickens.
The first night I was there
I saw the women pick up the milk pails
to go out to milk the cows.
The men ordered me to stop,
milking was women's work.
They dried and canned vegetables.

The Five Mile School was located on Five Mile Creek off the Mizpah River, five miles from the Powder River. The school building was in a bad state of disrepair when I took the job as teacher, but at Christmas time the community joined forces and fixed it up. A pot-bellied stove furnished heat, but before the building was repaired, the water bucket at the back of the room regularly froze. When I returned sixty-two years later, I could not find the location as floods had swept the ground entirely away.

◆ ◆ ◆

The food was good,
but I was tired of the taste of sagebrush in
        the wild game they killed.
The first night all the big boys
who had given so much trouble
        to the previous teachers
came  and wanted me to go swimming
in the big pool on Mizpah Creek.
        I was frightened.
        What would they do to me
        when I was naked in the water?
One boy, who had failed his eighth grade tests three times,
        was a year older than I.
        But I went with them
and splashed and dove like one of them
        and they liked me.
The next day they all arrived at school.
I decided to be one of them,
to play "Pom pom pull away" and "prisoner's base,"
but when they filed in and filled the double seats,
        I became their teacher.
There was no wood for the big stove
so we went out among the creekside cottonwoods
        and gathered firewood.
The mud chinking had fallen from the log sides,
so we mixed mud and straw and chinked the cracks.
I tried to make their days happy
as my mother did when she taught me.
We started the day with my reading from an
        interesting book.
We sang, and I was later to find a reed pump organ
        in a deserted rancher's house,
so our singing sounded less like an animal chorus.
Nearby in a solitary homestead

lived a mourning widower
whose wife had died and he lived in solitary loneliness.
He had been a professional violinist.
I had always wanted to be a violinist.
I bought a violin from a mail order catalogue for fifteen dollars
        and he taught me to play.
        The oldest girl in the eighth grade
        also decided to take lessons from him,
        and we would play duets together.
The first school board meeting was filled with tension.
        The members all carried guns
        except Mrs. Shook and me.
        One angry member pulled the fur cap
        down over the face of another member.
In the great poverty they had, there was much quarreling.
They cut each other's barbed wire fences,
        poisoned each other's cattle,
        and there had been four unsolved murders.
I had been janitor in a crafts shop
and watched them make flowers out of paper and wire,
so I bought some wire and paper
and invited all the ladies of surrounding homesteads
        to come on a Friday afternoon
        and make paper flowers.
Soon their poor houses, often papered with old
        magazines,
were ablaze with flowers even God hadn't thought of.
Soon we had programs and dances.
A lonely woman with bad teeth
was in love with the violinist.
        He paid her no attention.
She said, "I'm going to the river and drown myself."
He went to the corner of the room, picked up an axe,
and said, "The creek's frozen over, you will have to

cut a hole!"
When the winter came
it was good we had chinked the logs.
It was so cold we sat around the big stove
with our coats over our shoulders.
The water bucket in the corner of the room
                would freeze.
                Christmas came.
                We had a Christmas pageant.
One of the wise men, who later became a kleptomaniac,
stole his grandmother's snow shoes
and threw them in the creek.
I made the long Christmas journey home.
A terrible snow storm came.
I had to delay my return for a week.
                The only way I could get back
                was to make the journey by horseback.
It was the longest thirty-five miles I ever experienced.
                In ten hours through deep snow,
                I only saw one living person.
When I returned, they proudly led me to the schoolhouse.
They had laid in a supply of coal,
which was better than soft cottonwood for heat.
They had painted the interior a bright clear yellow
and had chinked the logs with cement to
replace the mud and straw the pupils had put in.
When the snow was deep on the ground,
                a hot chinook wind came.
                I heard a huge roar
                and looked up the Canyon Creek.
                I saw a wall of snow and water
                twenty feet high come roaring down.
I told the children, "Grab your coats and cross the
                bridge before it gets here!"
I grabbed my things and raced the wall of water

to the footbridge I used to get to the Shooks.
          At the conclusion of the term
          we had a hearty picnic and program.
The school board met and offered me a twenty dollar
raise to my eighty dollar salary.
They couldn't see how I could refuse them.
No one in that community made so much money.
My first graders could read, write, and add.
          Everyone had passed.
Pat Ogren, who was older than I and had been in the
          eighth grade three times,
and Alice Mallet, who used to play the violin with me,
both passed their eighth grade state examinations.
But I was off to college again with a small savings.

*September 1988*

# Shorty

When I had to ride horseback
the thirty-five miles to my teaching job,
John selected Shorty—a stocky quarter horse.
He had been castrated when he was full grown
and had the stocky muscular build of a stallion.
     His gait was slow
as he plowed through the knee-deep snow.
At noon I stopped by a pine stump
and gave him the small sack of oats I carried,
and I ate my lunch.
It was eleven at night when we arrived.
I think it was a week before
I could get the bow out of my legs.
I could only ride Shorty on weekends.
He would always try to buck me off
     but he never did.
Will Shook would ride one of his polo ponies
     and I would ride Shorty.
We would comb the distant hills and canyons
for the remains of homesteads that the
cattlemen or sheep men had run off
in a terrible war because
sheep ate the grass too close, but cows
did not harm the native pasture.
How many were killed, how many left with broken hearts?
One day, Shorty vanished. A neighbor said he had seen him
and an old grey mare headed south down Powder River.
Will and I saddled up our horses
     and went in pursuit.
We found them twenty miles south
ambling along, side by side.
We caught them and tied them up.
We stopped at a local ranch house,
knowing we could share what they had.

They had fried eggs and potatoes
and homemade bread with tart plum jelly.
We arrived home just as the stars came out.
Shorty never ran away again.
I guess he wanted one last romantic fling.

*September 1988*

The North Cottonwood Community Club met monthly during the winter,
taking turns meeting at members' houses. This 1921 meeting was held at my
parents' house. Generally, men discussed new methods of farming and the
women discussed subjects such as canning and sewing.

# The Blizzard

Mrs. Baker struggled through the deep snow
      to the schoolhouse
from her home two blocks away.
She said the operator of the telephone party line
      said, "A terrible storm is coming.
      Send the children home."
We put on our heavy winter coats
and stocking caps and woolen mufflers
      to cover our faces
to keep us from breathing the freezing air.
We already were wearing winter underwear with drop seats,
two shirts, two pairs of overalls,
and two pairs of socks.
Our overshoes were black and heavy.
The storm hit suddenly. There were great swirls
      of snow
      so that we could barely see.
John, twelve, broke the storm.
I, nine, came next clinging to his coat tails,
and Richard clung to mine.
Often Richard would fall and start to cry.
We would stop and carry him for a bit.
Suddenly I remembered the story
of relatives in the great blizzard of '98
who were out with a small child in a sled.
A great blizzard came and the horses
floundered and could not move.
The parents lay down in the straw of the sled,
put the child between them,
and covered themselves with a blanket.
In the morning searchers found them and their
      horses were frozen stiff,
but between the frozen bodies of the parents
      lay the sleeping child.

In their death they had saved her.
I was sure it was going to happen to us,
that they would find us all frozen stiff.
But out of the heavy swirling snow
our sister Myrtle appeared as an angel on horseback.
Richard was put behind her saddle,
John clung to the horse's tail,
and I clung on to his coat tails.
The horse broke the trail wind and made a path.
After a mile of struggle we arrived home.
No stove was ever warmer,
      no light so bright.
Mother put our feet and hands,
which were stiff, in warm water.
This she should not have done,
she should have placed them in cold water
and let them thaw out gradually.
Now that I am old, my hands tingle and become
      stiff on a cold day.
Why can't they forget that terrible blizzard?

*September 1988*

# The Magic Place

We called it the "Funny Place."

There was a strip of land
along the north side of our homestead.
It had been placed there by the surveyors
to allow for the meridian line,
and so no one owned it.
I was sad because it did not belong to us.
On it was a windswept hill
where the fierce winds had hollowed out
and uncovered the sandy beach from
an ancient sea that had once covered this
      barren land.

In it were the treasures for our young minds.
Whole skeletons of fish that crumpled in our hands
and tiny seashells that we would cup in our hands.
The glistening white sands were warm against our
      young bodies
and if no girls were there we would take off our
      clothes
and romp and play and dream of the great ocean
that our lives would take us to.

At the mouth of this treasured hollow
was a clump of thorny buffalo berry bushes,
pale green thorny little trees with tart tiny
      berries.
We would place our picnic blankets under them
and beat the branches of these small trees
and collect the tart berries to take home
to our mother who would combine them with
chokecherries to make jelly and wine.

Alas, seventy years were to exact their toll.
I returned to the blessed hollow,
but it was no more.
The same winds that had revealed its magic to us
had filled it up and only the same barren hill
　　　　was there.
But the winds of time could not erase
the beauty of our childhood.

# The Pretty Place

It was a very long walk
to our pretty place of dreams.
In this low hollow was a place of wonder
    and enchantment
by some forgotten miracle.

It was a place where wondrous plants would grow.
Here we found a dogwood bush with pale white flowers.
Crisp green ferns peered out from under the trees.
Climbing clematis vines with pale pink flowers
would festoon the trees around them.

My mother would transplant the clematis
and the ferns for her house and those of her neighbors.
She had a green thumb, they only seemed to grow for her.
There were chokecherry trees
with their tiny cherries hanging in clusters.

My father said if we ate them
and then drank milk, we would die,
like his childhood friend, Bobby.

There was a clump of wild plum trees.
Four of them were tart and prickey.
One of them had very sweet fruit.
The plums were fine for eating.
We called it the "sugar plum tree!"
We would pick the fruit and
take it home for my mother to make wine and jelly.
We would sometimes find currants, gooseberries,
        and serviceberries.

I always felt sad because the pretty place
was just over the line from our homestead.
It would have been a perfect place
        to build a house.

# The Honyonker Family

Many poor families that settled on a homestead
        were called "Honyonkers."
        I never knew why.
There was one family with five children
that lived in a two-room tarpaper shack
        on the section behind ours.
The father was a section hand
        working six days a week,
repairing the ties and steel of the railroad track.
Each Saturday night he would walk the eight miles
to be with his family before he walked back
        Sunday evening.
One day we met with these other children
        out by the "pretty place."
We were bragging about our mother's Sunday dinner,
        the best meal of the week.
The other children said, "I guess we will have
        potato soup again."
Their mother was big and fat,
but as she got fatter, we knew there was a
        baby on the way.
One morning the oldest boy came running.
He said, "Ma is in terrible pain."
Mother told John to saddle up a horse
and go to a neighbor that had a party line.
They gave a general ring (four longs on the
        crank telephone),
and all the women came rushing in their horse
        and buggies,
armed with clean sheets, old baby clothes,
and food for the family.
The children were sent outside
so they could not hear the screams and moaning.
When the baby was delivered and lay

sleeping in clean blankets beside his mother,
she lay reading a Sears and Roebuck catalogue.
She pointed to a bright silk dress
and said, "Some day I'll have a dress like that!"

*August 1988*

Homestead shack in winter.

# The Kitchen Stove

It was one of the first times I had seen my
      mother cry.
The hot coal fire had burned a hole in the side
      of the stove
and smoke and ashes were pouring out.
I ran to get my father.
He tried to stop my mother's tears.
He said, "How much money can we get together?"
There were two cans of cream
fresh from the noisy cream separator.
He had four sacks of wheat that he had saved for
      planting.
There was a few dollars in Mother's grocery jar.
Each of us had a few coins we had treasured away.
Together we got together the twenty-two dollars
for the shiny black stove Mother looked at
      so longingly
      in the Earling Burt Store.
Father hitched up the horses to the lumber wagon,
      and left for town.
He did not get back until after sundown.
We listened intently as the stars came out
for the jangling of the horses' harness.
      He came, smiling happily.
By the light of the smoking kerosene lamp,
      we saw the stove,
shiny and black with a high warming oven
and two shelves for the coffee pot.
It took all of us to lift it from the wagon,
and when we had it in the house,
we all admired its glossy nickel trim.
He pulled from his pocket a bag of candy.
He said, "I had twenty-five cents left over,
so I brought you some candy.

You can divide it amongst the five of you."
We liked the candy, but we liked the stove better.
We were happy our mother had quit crying.

*August 1988*

In 1917, while our mother and other women made bandages from clean
sheets, we hunted for discarded woolens to make an afghan. We washed and
unraveled old socks, mittens, sweaters, mufflers—every bit of woolen
material we could find—and knitted the yarn into squares. We pieced the
squares together to make an afghan for the soldiers in France.

# The Outhouse

When a homesteader finished building his house,
the next thing he built was the outhouse.
If he was a bachelor he made a single hole,
        if married, two holes.
Sometimes, if he had children, there might be
        three or four.
The greatest number I knew
was for a family with twenty-four children
whose name, strangely enough, was "Shitley."
        They had eight holes.
One day in school I was naughty.
The teacher said, "I am going to whip you."
She had followed me to the outhouse,
but no woman would enter a man's outhouse.
She said, "I'll wait, the smell will drive you out."
The smell did, but she didn't spank me.
Mrs. Schye was visiting the Carey Ranch.
They didn't have a door on their outhouse
and a group of cowboys rode by
and saw Mrs. Schye with her skirts up,
sitting there in great embarrassment.
Mr. Carey had just bought a new Studebaker.
Mrs. Schye said, "It's a pity people can buy
        a new car
        and can't afford a door on the privy!"
Women didn't like to go the outhouse
        if any man was looking.
What agony they must have endured waiting for
        the coast to clear.
When the homesteaders would abandon their failing
        homesteads,
neighbors would vandalize their houses for windows
        and lumber,
but the outhouse always stood, a smelly monument.

There were a lot of outhouse jokes.
The first one I heard was when I was eight:
The farmer's wife had cleaned her clothes with gasoline.
She threw the gasoline down the toilet hole.
Her husband came and, while sitting smoking his pipe,
     threw a match beneath him.
There was a terrible explosion.
He was thrown many feet in the air,
     and the building was destroyed.
He dazedly shook himself and said,
     "It must be something I et!"

*September 1988*

# Foxy

When December came
the snow banks were high,
the temperature was often forty degrees below,
and John and I could hardly make
the eight-mile trip to high school,
so we moved into town.
Dad could only find a tiny four-room house,
but it had a barn
so we could bring along chickens and a milk cow.
John, Richard, and I slept on a couch
      in the living room.
Edgar slept on the leaves of the dining table.
Mother and Dad had a tiny bedroom
and the kitchen was so small we could hardly move.
We endured this until planting.
When the rest of the family, except Mother and I,
      moved back to the homestead,
our next door neighbors moved away
and we could live in that larger house.
They left behind an old fat fox terrier.
As she had been deserted, she clung to me.
When I went to school, she went also
and sat on the school porch steps
until the sound of the school bell let us out.
I was two years younger than others in the class,
and because I was brighter, I was often lonely.
Foxy was my only friend.
She waddled like a fat old lady when we hiked,
but stopped to smell at any intriguing spot.
In the spring the local dramatic group
asked me to play a juvenile role.
Foxy decided she would be in every scene with me.
She was the star of the show.
One night Jim Anderson closed the door

on the stage after my entrance
and Foxy bit him on the ankle.
When the play ended
the other actors said if there was another play
Foxy couldn't be in it
because she got all the attention
and always spoiled their major scenes.
In June we moved back to the homestead.
Foxy was very sad and lonely.
She found herself a shady spot
under a big tree by the buffalo wallow
and lay all day looking at the water.
I took food to her,
and she would look at me with sad affection.
One morning she died, sleeping with her head
            between her paws.
I think she was like an old worn-out actress
dreaming of her days in the spotlight.

*September 1988*

# The Light in the Window

Mother always left a kerosene light
burning in the kitchen window.
Our house stood on a high hill.
She said it might make a lost traveler
      find his way.
One night when she put us all to bed
      in the laddered loft,
      she sat reading.
She always said she kept her mind alive
      by reading all she could.
It had been raining, and she heard the plop of
      horse's hooves
in the soft gumbo soil around the house.
The sound of the horse's hooves stopped
and the handle of the locked door
started to turn back and forth.
She shouted, "Who is it?"
      but no answer came.
The door knob on the door turned back and forth.
      She called us four children;
we hurried down and watched the door knob turn.
      We each called, "Who is it?"
Finally we heard the sound of horse's hooves dying away.
In the morning we found the hoof tracks.
We never knew who our late hour visitor was.
We only spent the summer making the homestead our own,
but left with the first snow.
Mother always left a supply of dry food
when we left for the city,
and the woodbox full beside the stove.
When we returned in the spring,
she always found more food than she had left in the fall.

*September 1988*

# The Cleaning Woman

Sometimes, when we would have a good crop,
Mother would hire Mrs. L to help her.
Mrs. L never stopped talking.
She talked about everybody, every thing,
          every which way.
One time to stop her from talking,
Mother asked, "How is your brother doing?"
Mrs. L, "Oh just fine. Last week he joined
          the Knights of Syphilis."
Mother said, "I hope he recovers."
          Mrs. L wondered why.
Another time, Mother asked how her daughter
          was doing.
She said, "Very poorly, she has diarrhoea
          in her teeth."
Mother said, "It must be hard to be around her."
Mrs. L said, "Her breath is so bad, no one
          can stand her."
Mother said, "No wonder."

*September 1988*

# The Wonderful Life of a Young Boy

When we were young and became noisy in the house
Mother would say, "Go outside and play."
We had no toys or any made things to play with.
We would take a rope and lasso a young calf
and ride it and pretend we were rodeo cowboys.
We could play cowboys and Indians.
I didn't like to be an Indian and always lose.
Our greatest fun was finding interesting things.
Our pockets would become full of treasures.
When Mother did her Monday wash,
she took these beautiful things
from our weekly issue of dirty bibfront overalls
and threw them out.
The things we found on the ancient prairie
would soon be forgotten.
A young boy sees things adult people cannot see
because adults are looking for specific things.
A young boy looks at everything.
We found arrows. One time we found them in a bunch.
We did not know that an Indian in the olden days
would take his best arrowheads
and place them around a stake
as a prayer for a big hunt.
Mountain sheep had once been many in the land,
but the early cattlemen killed them all off.
We found a skull of one whose two horns
had grown together and stuck out in front.
We had found a unicorn.
One day when searching for cattle
I saw a piece of bone sticking out of the dirt
twelve feet from the upper grass.
I climbed the bank and found a jawbone.
An old man said it was the jawbone of a camel.
A camel on these barren hills?

One day brother John came home with a gun.
It was a simple gun with just a barrel
and a little pan and a tiny hole into the barrel.
We figured you had to light a match
to make the gun go off.
A man who carried a gun like this,
how did he make it go off
if he had no matches?
We made a picket stake out of it
to keep the tethered horses from wandering off.
Sometimes we would find a piece of glasslike stone
and in it were ferns and trees.
These were valuable stones later made into jewelry.
When Mother would see a horse and buggy
coming down the distant road,
she would say, "Go call some chickens."
We would run them down, wring their necks,
dip their bodies in scalding water, remove their feathers,
and cut them up.
Sometimes in their gizzards
we would find bright gizzard stones.
No one told us the chickens found sapphires.
Down by the North Cottonwood School
was a high sandstone cliff
with a giant cave in the center.
We called it the "wolf den."
It was the only real wild animal we knew,
but on the inside were great claw marks,
the claw marks were an inch wide
and the paw that made it was ten inches across.
How was I to know that it was the den
of a giant sloth—a grass-grazing animal
of ten thousand years ago?
In these broad plains were the white clay cones

left from an ancient eruption.
Since there were no trees
eagles often made their nests on them.
But soon the ranchers had killed the eagles
because they thought they killed young lambs.
One night I was searching for the cows.
I climbed on one of these white cones
and brushed aside the deserted eagle nest
and dug into the soil beneath it.
There were the remains of an ancient fire.
Had this been a signal fire, or a place of worship?
One day I found a long white spear point,
a treasure.
I somehow knew that it was a rare find.

*September 1988*

Primitive transportation in the horse and buggy days.

# The Hired Man and the Mail Order Bride

Our hired man was a short, stocky, happy man.
    He had been born with an arm cut short
by cruel nature, the left arm, at the elbow.
He worked hard and dug our first well
    below Gumbo Flat.

He had a brother, happy, dark, and small, who
    nature had deprived of his full mental sense.
He relied upon his one-armed brother for support.

They had a homestead with a few sparse acres
where they built a two-room tar paper shack.
The elder man was lonesome,
    and he found a catalogue of women
    who were looking for a mate.

He sent pictures of another man with another farm
    to a woman in another state.
She likewise sent him pictures of her when she was very young.
She came to what she thought was a romantic western ranch
and with her, many possessions, elegant furniture,
    polished silver and china.

She was an old woman searching for a romance it
    seemed she had never had.
She found no close neighbors but my gentle Aunt Vedah.
She gave my aunt an ancient beer tankard,
which I still have,
And left to go back to a lonesome old age.

The brothers still were lonesome—
and in another catalogue they found pictures
　　　　of two handsome women who wanted to
　　　　　　　marry brothers.
　　　They came from Chicago,
　　　overly perfumed, overly painted,
　　　fat and overdressed, and worn
　　　from long nights in a brothel.

They took from the brothers their small savings
　　　　and bought all the cheap trinkets
　　　　our little town could offer.
The brothers were left minus their little savings
and came limping into the drugstore where I worked
to buy all the patent medicines that we had
for men who had contracted a venereal disease
　　　　and were ashamed to tell their doctor.

*July 1988*

# Lillian and Rose

Rose was the oldest of eight girls.
      They were named after flowers.
When the last one came
my grandmother said they should have named her Cactus.
Maybe it would stop any more from coming.
Rose was like a young flower
      that matured too soon.
Lillian was soft brown-skinned,
      with soft curly hair.
Her parents did not want to admit
that there was black blood
      in their family.
Each day when old "17"
      came in promptly at 3:17
      they met at the station
      giggling and posturing.
They hoped some lonesome traveling man
would notice them and perhaps
buy them a meal or an ice cream soda.
One night they went to a country dance
      at the Hay Creek School.
Out in the badlands by the dry Hay Creek
      they met two brothers,
tall in size, broad of shoulder,
but bland of face.
Out behind the school in the dusty sagebrush
      they seduced the girls.
A month later when their periods did not come
someone told them if they took mercury bichloride
      it would cause an abortion.
They came into the drugstore when the druggist was gone
      and bought a bottle from me.
When he returned I told him of their purchase.
He said, "My God, they will be dead in a month!

Get the doctor and go get them!"
In the dusty back room of the store
the doctor and the druggist pumped their stomachs.
They screamed and yelled, but it caused an abortion.
Lillian in her imagined shame
married the homeliest man in town,
an old bachelor with thick slobbering lips.
Rose married a wealthy young man
when he was recovering from a divorce.

*July 1988*

# Violet

The violets grew soft, blue, and tender
in the shady places of the barren west.
Violet was the fourth daughter.
She became a woman when she should have played
  with dolls.
She used to come to the drugstore,
hoping someone would buy her an ice cream soda.
One night she came in with a tall dark cowboy
who wore his high-heel boots with jangling
  spurs.
They clanked as he crossed the floor.
He took Violet to the jewelry case
and told her she could have anything in it.
She selected the most garish glass beads
and put them on like she was a queen.
A month later she came into the store.
She was sad and wouldn't eat the ice cream she loved.
The cowboy left town—her mother scolded her.
In childish shame she tried to give herself
  an abortion with a hat pin. She died.
They buried her up on the barren hill.
  Her father came in and said,
   "I couldn't give her much in life,
   but I was able to buy the silk dress she wanted."
    She was buried in it.

*July 1988*

# Buck and Bill

My father needed two more horses.
Frank and Roaney were not strong enough
to pull the heavy farm machinery.
He went to a horse auction with little money.
There were two horses at the end of the auction
        that no one wanted.
Bill was born with a round hoof, like a club-footed
        child,
        but he was dark, sleek, and strong.
Buck had been damaged by a cut from a barbed
        wire fence
and had a stiff rear leg, but he was a glistening
        white.
        So my father got them cheap.
        They were good workers,
each trying to outdo the other.
Straining and struggling to the sweaty harness
they always seemed to be together.
        We never spoke of them as one.
They would always seem to graze together;
        perhaps in their mutual pain
they found comfort in the infirmities of the other.

*August 1988*

# Wood, Coal, Potatoes, and Corn

## Wood

Dad had gone away to work to get some
money because there had been little success
with crops except potatoes and corn.
Mother had been selected to teach
the North Cottonwood School
and she told John, 14, and me, 11, to go
to the Pine Hills to get wood for winter.
Dad had bought a lumber wagon.
Shiny and new, it had cost Dad three hundred dollars.
It was not completely paid for.
We hitched up Bill with the round hoof
and Buck with the stiff leg
and made the long bumpy trip
to the distant Pine Hills
where we hoped to poach for wood
upon a wealthy landowner's land.
On the way we passed the Youngs' deserted
　　　　　homestead shack.
Mr. Young had a wooden leg.
The Youngs had made the case the new leg came in
into a window flower box, now filled with dead plants
and an advertisement on the box to tell the world
of Mr. Young's accident.
We found a gate on the fence on the forbidden ground,
opened the gate, and went up a steep hillside.
The wagon slipped against a tree.
We tried to get it loose and could not.
We saw two neighbors going by
who had been poaching wood.
John asked them for help.
They refused us but gave John a heavy log chain
and with it we got the wagon off the tree.
It went bouncing down the hill

and cracked the frame.
John sat down and cried, afraid to tell Dad.
We loaded the wagon with rotting wood,
not much good for warmth
              but good for kindling.
As we started to leave we saw a little Christmas tree.
We knew we could put it in water
and it would keep until Christmas.
We returned home late, weary, and tired,
but we had a Christmas tree.

## Coal

We heated our house with the big coal stove,
              often red hot
              from the fresh lignite coal.
The coal mine was on the Frederickson's place
              four miles away.
Other farmers had stripped away
the overburden of earth with a horse-drawn sulky.
They had left a little uncovered coal
and so John with pick and shovel
managed to get some large chunks loose
and put them in a bushel basket
and between us we labored up the steep bank
and filled the lumber wagon.
We returned triumphant; we had
enough coal to keep us warm in winter!

## Potatoes

The telephone party line brought the news
to Mrs. Baker that there was a terrible storm coming.
She trudged to the schoolhouse
where Mother was teaching.
Mother sent us home to get the potatoes out of the ground

before the winter storm hit.
John hitched up the horses to the walking plow
and guided them down the long rows
where we had picked potato bugs in early summer.
There had been a rain the night before,
the ground was wet, cold, and clammy.
I had to pick up the potatoes
and put them in a gunnysack.
I could not wear gloves, they were too cumbersome,
and I would beat my hands against my body
to keep them from freezing.
The potatoes did not freeze
and we dragged the full sacks
and stored them in the cool basement
where we also kept the coal in winter.
I've always loved potatoes, they seem the staff of life,
but I remember that freezing autumn day
        when I picked them.

## Corn

There had been a poor crop of wheat that year,
but there had been a fair crop of corn.
The stalks stood in dry rustling rows,
waiting to have the dry ears of corn removed
        from their dead bodies.
John made a husker with a short piece of leather
and a nail to help remove the husks.
He put a backboard on the lumber wagon,
and we would husk the corn and throw it against the
        backboard
as the horses moved slowly down the rows.
How proud we were when the job was finished.
Some corn we ground for cornmeal,
some went to feed the horses, cows, and pigs,

and the soft white curry cobs
ended up as firewood in the kitchen stove
or in the smelly outhouse
to be used as toilet paper when the mail catalogue
          was gone.

I grew this corn as a 4-H Club project.

# Trilogue
# For Three Strangers in a Strange Land

In the early days of the opening West, strangers, mostly from England, would come to the local post office each month and receive a check. They were paid by their families to stay away. I don't know what impropriety they had done that caused their families to send them away. It was perhaps their search for freedom that brought them to the untamed early West.

## Ode to a Great Lady

When she was young and titled
she had been presented at the courts of Europe.
Great balls, great concerts had been her food.
She landed at a barren cattle ranch amongst the cattle,
the barren badlands, and the mournful coyote.
When she would make the harsh journey into town,
clad in a faded print dress and a wilted cowboy hat,
she would wear her jewels from the faded past:
great square emeralds and Egyptian scarabs
in fine gold settings.
She would go to the lobby of the hotel
where there was a noisy upright piano
and play Chopin and "Money Musk"
for delighted listeners.
Sometimes in the harsh cold winters
she would come and stay in town.
And coach our struggling dramatic group in plays
and regale us with stories of great operas and great plays.
One night she died
and the local undertaker brought her in dead,
but always a lady,
sitting up regally in the back seat of a chugging Model T.
He embalmed her body and put her in a white casket

and placed her all alone in the small church.
A few people came to her funeral.
There was no one to pump the organ for the organist,
and so behind a screen, I pumped the organ,
sometimes with tears for the great lady
who would soon be forgotten and buried
in the lonesome hillside grave.

# The Astute Professor

He was tall and stately, wore a monocle
even on the long journey from his isolated ranch.
He raised horses for the cavalry.
They were beautiful horses, and he cared for
them as though they would perform in a steeplechase.
He called his ranch the "Fiddleback" and that
was also his brand—I thought that when I grew up
I would like to have a brand like that.
One day my brother John and I, while
looking for a lost horse, stopped at his lonely ranch,
log cabins, red, red gravel roofs, great corrals.
He came to the door with quilted smoking jacket
and slippers and led us to a bench filled with
great books and mementoes of another world.
He liked to talk to Mother because she knew
Greek and Latin and great literature.
At one time he was a witness in court,
and the bigoted judge said,
"What are your educational qualifications?"
He answered, "I was a professor of Greek at Oxford."
The World War came and the cavalry horses could not
survive against the awful machines of war.
The government bought no horses,
and so he turned his horses loose where they

wandered the badlands in great wild herds.
He died and his soul was free to wander
the lonesome hills with his horses.

## The Sheepherder

He arrived on the slow afternoon local train
carrying with him a small valise and precious bagpipes.
From the noisy sounds of a nearby saloon
he knew that he would find a job.
He was tall, dark, and strong
and had a rich Scottish burr in his speech.
How would anyone know that this strong man
was the son of a Scottish chieftain.
He found a job herding sheep for a rich rancher.
He lived in a sheep wagon,
a covered wagon with a stove in one end and
a bed in the other and cupboards along the side.
He was given a dog, a gentle Scottish côllie
who was to comfort him in his lonely isolation, and
a team of horses who were always tethered
or hobbled to keep them from wandering off.
They would move the wagon to a place of new grass.
Two thousand sheep were his constant companions.
Once a month the supply wagon would find him
and give him dry supplies and canned goods.
The dog kept the coyotes away at night,
rounded up stragglers when they moved,
and slept beside him in comfort at night.
Three days out of every month he would be relieved
and go into town and squander his monthly salary
of one dollar a day and board.
And when the ladies of the night and the saloons
had gotten his meager pay,
he would return to the silent loneliness of the prairie.

Often in the night
he would get out his bagpipes and wear his kilt
and march around with no one to see but the
skulking coyote.
Here he would dream of Scottish moors,
battles long forgotten, and his valiant ancestors.
When lambing came, he would bring us
the barn lambs whose mothers had died
and we would feed them on a bottle and
watch them play and gambol.
Whatever became of him I do not know,
but his remittance check would come in
and nobody came to claim it.
Perhaps he found the peace he wanted
in the silent loneliness of the prairie.

*August 1988*

# The Day that Richard Came

It was just past my third birthday
when there was a great stir in the house.
Elizabeth and John were sent to stay at Bakers;
Edna, the oldest Baker girl, came
and left all the barbed wire gates open
to speed the doctor in his chugging Ford;
and Nanny Richardson had come.
She had been my mother's hired girl
in our more affluent days before our
       homestead years.

I was placed in the surrey just outside
       the kitchen door
and given an orange to eat.
A piece fell on the ground, and the cat
came and smelled it and would not eat it.
I wondered why the rare orange I liked
       so much
would not be liked by the cat.

From the bedroom I could hear my mother
screaming in pain.
I wept because I could not bear
that my dear mother should suffer like that
and I could not go and comfort her.
Soon the doctor came in his noisy Model T,
and the cries stopped.
And then there was a hubbub of washing
       bloodied sheets.

Soon I was brought in,
and my mother lay smiling with a baby cradled
        in her arms.
"This is your new brother," she said.
"I have named him Richard
after my dear friend who has come so many miles
to care for me."
I did not know where babies came from.
I thought dear Nanny had brought it with her.

*July 1988*

# The Day that Edgar Came

My mother had become so large
that she could not hold me on her lap.
My brother John had told me it was not fat
but my mother had a baby in her.
I wondered how it got there
but John could not tell me that.
Grandma Broman and Aunt Vedah had
come to stay.
I thought they had come to celebrate
my birthday two days before.

My father said, "Go down and open all
the gates to the barbed wire fences.
And then go down and play in the gumbo patch."
It had rained that night and from the moist clay
we made figures of animals and machines.
Soon my father came and said,
"You must go to Sidey's Spring and get more water."

John was nine and Elizabeth eleven.
They harnessed and hooked old Frank and Roanie
to the stoneboat.
A stoneboat is just some planks bolted together,
and on it were two barrels (one of them leaked).
We dragged the stoneboat the dusty mile
and hurried to fill the barrels from the clear,
cool water of Sidey's Spring.
We did not stop to catch the frogs that we sometimes did
and have my mother cook them, jerking in the
frying butter. We did watch sundogs swimming around.
We hurried home, the water jostling in the barrels.

There were white sheets on the clothesline,
and my mother lay smiling with a tiny baby at her side.
We asked his name.
My father said, "I have named him George Edgar
after my uncle from whom I inherited a little
money that made it possible to come to this homestead."
I wondered how he could have been so cruel
to place us in this barren land.

We called him Edgar.  He was our loving jewel, our baby.
The first fight I ever had was when Elmer Schye
said he looked like a frog.

I was five years old when Edgar was born.

# My Mother's Ring

Sometimes when I am sad
I wear upon a thin gold chain
my mother's loving ring around my neck.
It is so small—three bright red garnets
and eight small pearls.
Her hands were small and tender,
yet I could see her hands
in the lye-soaked water, scrubbing
out dirt with a rough tin board,
or kneading bread and mixing cakes
she served to those she loved,
baking them on the hot coal stove.
Five children she bore in her body
and to each she gave her love and care.
And in the classroom where she taught us,
her hands caressed the great loved books
she read to us,
with all the excitement they had brought to her.
She taught us, fed us, and caressed us
and sent us on our way,
knowing that her love was our protection.
And somehow when I am deeply sad,
the little ring brings back to me
the glory, beauty, and wonder that
she passed on with her small hands,
wearing the small gold ring.

Mother, Elizabeth, and I.

# My Father's Hands

When he lay in that harsh box
where he would return to the soil
    that he loved so well,
I could not look upon his face
    for when his eyes were closed
    he was not there.

    I could only see his hands,
still strong and beautiful in death.
    I don't think he ever touched me
      except to spank me
or to say good-bye with a stilted handshake.
    I know he could only show his love
    through working hard to feed those
      his blood brought into the world.

How hard he worked for seven decades,
    plowing with a single walking plow
      or bundling grain or mining coal.
    Because he had no father
    I don't think he ever knew
      how great he was.
    He always took the lesser road,
thinking he was not worthy to ask for more.

    I wish the curtain of stilted manner
    had not always hung between us,
and I could have kissed him and have
him say the three loved words, "I love you,"
    or place his arms around my shoulders—

But I could only see his fine hands,
      silent and cold.

Henry Beardsley, circa 1932.

# The Wrath of God

Preacher Williams came on his monthly rounds
     to the schoolhouse.
He preached that, because the Jews were God's
     chosen people
and the Egyptians were mean to them,
God sent seven plagues against the Egyptians.
I knew only one Jew— sweet, gentle Mrs. Marks,
who always gave Christmas presents to all
     the children in the school.
I thought she gave them because Jesus was also a Jew.
We had not wronged any Jews, so why had God
     given us so many plagues?
Grasshoppers would fill the sky with their
     roaring wings.
They would eat all the growing plants,
and Dad would collect the grasshoppers for chicken feed,
     our only source of meat and eggs.
The cut worms came and newly planted crops
     lay wilted in a day.
The hail storms would come suddenly
     out of a blackened sky
     and beat the crops down
and mother had us hold pillows against
the big front window that was her pride.
Blackleg came and the cattle were dying.
The neighbors gathered their herds and vaccinated them
     on section one below our house.
Pig cholera came and the last pig died.
Horse distemper came and the two best horses
     lay stinking in the pasture.
The drought came and where once was knee-high grass
     now was dry and barren ground.
We had never hurt any Jews,
why was God giving us so many plagues?

# J. M.

J. M.'s parents died when he was a little boy.
He lived with his grandparents on a high hill
        in Bristol, England.
He watched huge ships with billowing sails
bringing cargo from all over the world.
One day, lonely and forgotten, he climbed aboard
        and became a cabin boy
and sailed all over the world.
Because no women were allowed on board,
he performed all the lowly duties women would perform.
When he was grown he entered the German Naval Academy,
but when he saw the Germans' warlike intent,
he left and then contracted tuberculosis and came
        west to seek a cure
on the barren plains of South Dakota.
His health returned and he married the farmer's daughter.
They had three daughters and three sons
        and made some money.
He came to eastern Montana where for a brief period
        nature was plentiful.
He never seemed to work, but he directed his sons
        and others while
his wife managed a huge household.
He gave ground for the new school close to his house.
His oldest daughter filed on a homestead
and in the winter taught the North Cottonwood School.
They said that when his wife was young
she had been plain and unattractive.
She loved babies, and since her youngest was twelve,
she would ask my mother to let me stay.
She spoiled me.  She let me sit on her lap
and smell her fresh starched bosom.  Soft and warm
and always smelling of fresh bread,
she was the most beautiful woman I knew.

I loved to stay, but one day my father
came to take me home. I hid under a bed
and he spanked me, and I heard a terrible quarrel
between my father and Mrs. J. M.
One day in Sunday School I heard J. M. singing bass
        in a rich round voice.
It was the first time I had heard someone sing a song
        with other than the melody.
I vowed I would learn to sing like him.
He would tell me names like the Catagat and
the Scagarrat and have me find them on a map.
Children never seem to listen to the stories of their parents;
        I was like a grandchild.
When the harsh years of drought came
with the depression that covered the land,
he went to town and opened a station to buy cream
        from the farmers,
but cream was the last product farmers could sell.
The milk cows could not seek out a few blades of grass
        in those desperate years.
The homesteaders left the farms they worked so hard to build,
going west in battered cars with few possessions
        like lemmings going to the sea.
I saw J. M. just before he died.
In my youthful forgetfulness I did not tell him
        how much I cared for him.
I saw Mrs. J. M. many years later.
She was a sweet, pretty old lady,
but she had forgotten all the beautiful past.

Mr. and Mrs. J. M. Baker

In 1927 the Ismay drugstore was the hub and meeting place in town. Elias Ayers was not only the druggist but also the undertaker, radio repairman (radios were just coming into use), justice of the peace, and head of the Masonic lodge. Here I am, behind the jewelry counter at the right, at age seventeen running the store while Elias took a month's vacation.

# Elias Ayers

Elias came west on one of the first immigrant trains.
His father filed a claim on a homestead north of town.
Elias had previously studied pharmacy in Wisconsin
      and went to work at T. J. Maddox's store.
T. J. had first built a frame building
along the wooden sidewalks of the emerging town,
but the front door was lower than the new cement sidewalk
so he built a new one—a fine building
with mahogany showcases, jewelry cases, and a
      cigar counter,
a marble ice cream fountain with a Tiffany bordered
      mirror behind.
Mr. Maddox had a sad divorce from his wife
      and sold the store to Elias.
Elias, who had passed his pharmacy exam,
made many of the medicines the local doctor prescribed.
Because I could not stand the eight-mile horseback ride
to the local high school,
my father asked Elias for a job for me.
He did not know it would change my life.
I did not like the barren ranch life,
where it seemed there was nothing
but lonesome tumbleweed blowing in the wind
and hungry cattle hunting for a blade of grass
and grasshoppers and cutworms that ate
      everything in sight
and howling coyotes baying in the night
and poverty and Mother's brave, sad tears.
It was a great gift to work for him.
He paid me five dollars for an unlimited week.
Each morning I would sweep the store, dust
the showcase, get ice from the ice house, crush
and mix it with salt for the ice cream fountain.
Elias would come when I had to go to school.
My heart would increase its beat when I saw him coming.

They say that a man's first love is his mother
and his second love may be his father or some
other man kind to him.
Elias had a retarded son my age, gentle and quiet,
but Elias gave me all the attention he would have
        given his son.
He taught me how to put up prescriptions, follow the
        metric scale,
roll pills, make salves, stuff capsules
and the nature of the many bottles on the shelves.
He taught me never to put up a prescription unless
I knew the nature of every ingredient.
And if I did not know, I would ask the doctor
        to come and fill his own.
I ordered new merchandise, collected past due accounts.
When I was fifteen he took a vacation for a month
and left me to run the store, which I was to do
        again and again.
There was no one to take care of the dead
        in this far-flung country
        so Elias studied embalming.
He would bring them in Mrs. Prindle's old Model T,
the dead sitting straight up, but covered with blankets.
He embalmed them and laid them out
in the back room of Mr. Maddox's old store,
a room filled with old dusty furniture
and caskets of many sizes.
I did not like to go in there
because of the smell of death and formaldehyde.
One day he heard there was an old horse-pulled hearse
for sale in the little town of Ekalaka.
It was black, with beveled glass and wavy ostrich plumes.
He bought and put it on a flatbed truck.
The dead were now escorted to the hilltop cemetery
        in one last defiant act.

He was worried that his embalming would not be good.
But Mr. Jarrat died and six weeks later
his enormous fat wife decided to dig him up
and ship his body to the place of his birth.
The embalming was complete.
Mr. Jarrat lay with his hands crossed
and a smile on his face.
The saddest case was when two boys
stole their father's dynamite and went to dynamite fish.
One was badly scarred, but the other one
        was blown to bits.
Elias wanted me to help him put the mangled
        pieces together for burial.
I vomited and told Elias that if ever he asked
        me to do that thing I would leave.
He was master of his Masonic lodge,
sometimes mayor, always justice of the peace.
He sang tenor in the church choir,
and when the town band was formed,
he learned to play the baritone horn.
I don't think he ever scolded me.
During the summer he paid me $125 a month.
It was a wage my father had never received in his
        lifetime.
I loved to act and was in three or four plays a year.
He allowed me to leave early,
and on Sundays I would lead the young people's group
and sometimes gave the sermon in church.
I felt guilty because I didn't want to be a farmer
or a cowboy. I didn't like dirt and cow manure.
So, if I had one person to thank for being what I am,
it would be Elias Ayers.
He respected and trusted me,
and I learned to respect and trust myself.

# Pussy Willow Grey

Our new neighbor had given us a dog named Bob.
     He attacked a little grey hen
and hurt her leg so she hobbled along.
They were going to kill her and eat her for supper.
     I loved her and wept bitterly.
So they said, "She is yours to keep."
I was only five—but I named her
     Pussy Willow Grey
     because she was so soft and grey,
like the early blooms of the willow in spring.
She was a dear friend.  I could talk to her,
and she would always answer with a gentle cluck
to assure me that the world was still alright.
We would take walks together,
and she would flutter after a jumping grasshopper.
     I would go to her roost at evening
     to see that she was there
happily sleeping with her head under her wing.
One night I went to say "goodnight" to her.
     She was not there.
I wandered over the dry prairie grass
until I found some little sad grey feathers.
She had wandered too far looking for grasshoppers.


*August 1988*

# Old Spot

Old Spot was the first milk cow
my father was able to buy.
A defeated homesteader was selling off his
        poor possessions
to go back from where he had come,
and he reported she was a good milker.
He did not say she was a mean old bitch.
When the first night came for the milking,
we waited anxiously outside the little barn door.
        I had been raised on canned milk,
and the thought of fresh milk was exciting.
All went well, the pail became full,
but with an angry swish of her tail across
        Dad's face
and a violent kick, she sent Dad sprawling out
        the barn door,
        the fresh milk all over him.
Dad emerged saying bad words;
he usually would not stoop to swearing.
We had no fresh milk that night.
Spot later quieted down.
She was to produce many calves,
which were the beginning of a large herd.
The cattle seemed to always find forage on the plain,
        and with a humming cream separator,
we were able to sell cream to trade for groceries.
        When times became worse and harsh,
there was no feed, and desperately, to avoid
        complete poverty,
John and I drove a herd of thirty cattle to the
        freight station.
We didn't get enough to pay the freight.
Spot and her many calves were among them.
Old Spot, in spite of her nasty disposition,
        had done her best.
She could not help the times.

# Barney

Animals, like people, seem to be born with
      set dispositions.
Barney, from birth, was always of a lovable
      nature.
Son of Spot, who did not have his gentle ways.
When he was a calf he let us ride him,
and when he was castrated he grew large and fat.
When we would go looking for the cattle on the
two section pasture
and were very tired, trying to avoid the cactus
that abounded in the harsh badlands,
Barney would let us ride him, sometimes double.
One day I came home trudging from the school
      two miles away
        and we had steak for dinner.
We rarely had meat as there was no refrigeration,
only the cool of the root cellar.
I asked, where did we get the meat?
No one had been to the May butcher shop in town.
My father said Mr. May came out from town
and killed Barney and took part of the meat for
      killing him.
I looked at the meat lying on my plate.
I could not eat the friend I loved.
I went out in the yard and threw up.

*August 1988*

# The Four Ducks

Mrs. Baker had given us six duck eggs.
We placed them under a brooding hen
and four downy ducklings emerged in quacking wonder.
We played with them, and they followed us
with quacking pleas.
They did not see any water except in their enameled pan.
When they were nearly full grown,
the four of us decided they should someday see real water.
My two brothers and a cousin and I climbed on our
bareback horses
to take them to Sidey's pond.
My little brother, Edgar, was left behind weeping
because he was too young to ride alone.
Each of us held a quacking duck under our arms
and rode with a sweating horse between our legs.
We galloped past the prairie dog town
where the moving sentinels scurried in retreat
and opened the gate to Sidey's pasture.
Sidey's pond was nearly full
from a recent summer cloudburst.
It was chest full of muddy water.
We chased the ducks and the ducks chased us.
We heard Mrs. Casey, in her noisy new Studebaker, coming.
So we all lined up, and as she passed
we bent and bared our little butts to her.
She thumbed her nose at us,
and so four wet boys caught four wet ducks,
and slippery on our horses' backs,
we rode home happy.
Our ducks had seen real water!

*1988*

# Bess and Butte

Bess was the first good mare
my father was able to buy.
She was plump and gentle,
a glistening sorrel with a gentle, amiable
        disposition.
My father took her to Joe Noll's stallion
        to have her bred.
When her birthing time was coming,
she went off to the badlands section of the
        ranch
and bore her pain all by herself.
Dad went to look for her and found her with a
        beautiful son
and came home leading her with her foal,
spindly legs wobbling, at her side!
We named her son "Butte"
as our name started with "B."
We named all our animals with names that started
with "B."
        Butte grew big and strong.
He did not resist when he was taught to wear the
saddle and the harness.
He was good in the field, trying to outpull the
        other horses.
He was a stern disciplinarian.
He could not stand other unruly horses,
and when brother John was breaking horses for
        the neighbors,
John would hitch them up with Butte.
If the other horse rebelled, Butte would lean over
and grab his neck with his teeth and shake him
and the other horse would quiet down.
When the drought and depression came
and horses were selling for three dollars

(they had been selling for
three hundred dollars),
John sold him for thirty dollars.
I hope he got a good home.

*August 1988*

The thrashing machine and steam engine were a cooperative venture of the community. It took many people to carry out all the activities which are now done by a singe combine. This photo shows the North Cottonwood Thrashing Crew in 1926. My brother John and I are on the extreme right. We were paid by the amount of bushels we completed. Some days we made as much as $5.00 working from sunrise to sunset.

# Princess

When my mother went looking for a homestead
        for my grandmother,
she met a shepherd whose sheepdog
            was a Scotch collie
            with five little puppies,
            a bright little animal whose ancestors
for centuries
had been companions to lonely sheepherders.
Mother brought a puppy home.
She became a member of our family
and went with us when we searched
            for cows and horses.
While we avoided the harsh cactus
            with our bare feet,
she would happily circle around us,
sniffing at gopher holes or chasing a rabbit
or stopping suddenly when she aroused a prairie chicken
            and heard the noisy flutter of her wings.
One day my mother put
            my little brother Edgar
            on a blanket out in the yard.
            Mother heard Princess barking loudly.
            She went out, and Princess
            was keeping her little body
between a slithering rattlesnake and the baby.
Sometimes she wandered off when she was in heat
            and found a neighbor's dog.
She once had five little puppies,
and since we could not feed any more dogs,
brother took the five squealing babies
and drowned them in a tub of water.
He buried them, but Princess found the grave.
She dug them up and tried to warm their
            little cold dead bodies.

She keened and sobbed over them,
licking the dry dirt from their tiny bodies.
There was another year of drought.
The war was on and there was work in a distant town.
We took Princess to our grandmother's ranch
            some miles away.
            Princess would not eat.
            She returned to the lonely homestead
            where she knew life and love.
            When we returned in the spring,
            the little body of Princess
            was curled up dead by the back door.
If there is a God who doesn't like dogs
            and will not let her in,
            I'll go looking for her.


*August 1988*

# Dan Patch

Horses have many gaits;
each is adapted to the time and place.
They go from walk, trot, canter, and gallop,
but some are blessed with another gait.
It is called "pacing."
Pacing horses are very rare.
A few can be taught with straps on their legs,
but to some few, the pacing comes naturally.
John was a horse trader, a good one.
One morning he started out
　　　leading a sickly calf
and came home with a team of harness horses.
One time he came home with a beautiful horse;
I don't know where brother John got him.
He called him Dan Patch after the famous horse
who made millions for his owners.
He, too, was black with white patches.
We always wrangled for the privilege to ride him.
John would take wild bucking horses
and teach them to be saddle horses.
We would ride each day to the high school
　　　seven miles away.
John would ride them the first week and I the
　　　next week.
I was never thrown, but they tried!
John had a gentle way with animals.
He seemed to be able to talk to them
and, by gentle strokes, tell them to trust him.
We rode that fall until the temperatures became
forty degrees below zero
and we had to walk beside our horse and beat our
　　　hands to keep from freezing.
I was relieved to have time to study my Latin and algebra
and the beautiful books that opened that
great mysterious world beyond the far horizon.

# Frank

Frank was a stocky loveable horse.
      He didn't walk, but ambled
      like a little old lady
browsing for bargains in a department store.
      Father had carried mail
and Frank would draw the mail cart
and stop while Dad took the mail inside.
But Dad got the homestead bug
and Frank was shipped west in a boxcar
along with the family surrey and furniture.
Dad slept in the boxcar with Frank
while our mother and the four children were in the
      immigrant coach behind,
      with the sound of crying babies,
      the smell of the smoky coal stove,
the odor of cigars and peeled oranges from the lunch
      basket,
and the sound of the hawker selling his wares.
When they reached the sprawling new town of Ismay,
the boxcar was unloaded, the wheels put on the surrey,
      and Frank was hitched up
      and we traveled the rutted road
      to the unfenced tar paper shack.
Shortly before it had been the home of buffalo.
When the wood from the pinehills had been stacked
      and dry groceries had been procured,
we could not find a place to hang the hammock.
There were no trees on that wind-swept plain.
The croquet balls did not roll on the gumbo flat.
The bantam chickens scurried wildly,
and our tiny French poodle
was only good for the children to put doll clothes on.
      Frank was the indispensable one.
My father plowed a furrow with the walking plow

over the bouncing hills so Mother
could drive old Frank to the North Cottonwood School
        where the Sunday school met.
Each week, sister Myrtle would saddle up old Frank
and go to town seven miles away for groceries.
There was no refrigeration, so everything was
        dry or canned.
One day the great rains came.
The bridge across the O'Fallon River washed out.
When Myrtle came to the swollen river,
she urged old Frank into the rushing water
and swam alongside him, hanging on to the saddle horn.
She got the necessary groceries and swam back,
bringing the canned milk for the baby,
        which was me.
One day, my mother in the barren loneliness
wanted to see my Aunt Nell just for friendly woman talk,
so she started out to visit Aunt Nell and Uncle Charley.
        They lived twenty miles away
        by a large butte.
With only that to guide them,
they started out with Myrtle at the reins.
There were no fences and no roads.
With three younger children in the back seat
and the little white French poodle keeping them company,
they passed great herds of sheep
and groups of frightened antelope running away.
After a short happy afternoon and
a huge meal, she started home.
She sighted Bracketts Butte,
and with only Frank plodding along,
they arrived home just as the stars came out.
Frank had done his duty well.
Frank didn't like to be caught in the morning

after he had spent the night feeding on the prairie grass.
Three little children would try to catch him.
He would let them get close and then run away.
My father, who had gone away to earn some money,
        had come home late that night,
walking the seven miles from the train station.
He came out of the prairie shack
        and yelled at Frank.
Frank stopped and went to the voice he loved.
I think he was hoping they could go back
to the slow peaceful mail route
and get away from the damn lonesome prairie.

*August 1988*

# Living Water

When the homestead settlers chose the half section
that the government had allotted them with
one hundred dollars and a three-year occupancy,
some were wise and chose a half section
that had a spring or pond or indication of water.
Some were famous for the quality of the water,
and people came for miles to drink of it.
My father hired Harold Vroman
to dig a well down by the buffalo wallow.
When he reached the water but also solid rock,
the water was too alkaline for use
and we had to seek water elsewhere.
We hauled it in barrels from Sidey's Spring
or Mr. McKee's well that he had dug on top a high hill
and with a windmill and cistern he had
flowing water to his house and barns.
The Sidey brothers had a flowing spring
that came out of a high bank,
and in the hillside dam, they made shelves
where rich creamy pans of milk were placed
to get the cream to make butter.
Brother John was to drill a well
near the original failure,
and they struck a vein of gushing artesian water.
J. M. Baker, the most successful farmer,
drilled two expensive wells on section eleven
and both became dry holes,
so he built a cistern to collect rain from the roof
and in dry times hauled water.
Mr. McKee decided to dig another well
in his cow pasture.
He hired a drifter—at one dollar a day—
  to dig it.
All alone in that deep dark hole,

gasses formed and he died.
It was the first death in that emerging community
       of brave people.
It was a strange quirk of fate
that the next two deaths in this dry land
       were from drowning.
The Osters were from Russia
but they spoke German.
They had selected a half section
which had a natural spring and pond.
Their six-year-old son fell in and drowned.
Mother took some of our outgrown clothes
       to bury the little baby in
and made a cross of blooming lilies
to place upon the tiny casket.
The Milwaukee Railroad had a dam
to water the sheep being driven to market.
To me it was a glorious body of water,
the largest I had ever seen,
but now I know it was just three acres.
Harold Stewart went to fight in the first World War.
How handsome he was in his khaki uniform.
One day on his return he went looking for his
       father's cattle.
When he came to the Milwaukee Dam,
he stripped and dove into the water and died.
The Ladies' Aid met and decided to start a cemetery.
Harold Stewart's father came with a lumber wagon,
borrowed our reed organ so there would be
hymns at his son's funeral.
The Ladies' Aid selected a spot on Carey's place
at a point that overlooked the North Cottonwood Valley,
and the neighbors dug a grave
and lowered his strong, young body into it.

How sad it was that in this dry land
the first three deaths were from drowning.
When in Sunday school
they sang about living waters,
I thought sadly how they sometimes
        brought death.

*August 1988*

Oscar Brackett in about 1912. The tall woman is Vedah
Broman Baker, the first switchboard operator.

# The Ladies' Aid Society

The homesteaders arrived in 1909 or 1910.
They had been urged by the large pictures
of free rolling prairies with knee-deep grass
  all for free.
The first thing they did was to build a school.
  J. M. Baker gave the land,
  and all pitched in to build it and
  erect a flagpole, swing, and teeter-totter.
The women gathered together to form a Ladies' Aid
  Society.
Usually an Aid Society helps a church.
There was a move to create a community club house,
but the women wanted a church,
so neither was ever built—the school was enough.
The Bakers and the Stewarts were Methodist.
The Schyes (Mrs. Schye had been Jewish) were Congregational,
the Fredericsons were Lutherans, a church my mother
had been raised in, but they were too stern
so she had joined the Dutch Reform Church.
Mrs. Marks, the tall handsome wife
  of the manager
  of the huge Diamond Ranch, was Jewish,
but she sent Christmas presents to all the children
  in the school.
There didn't seem to be much difference in any of them.
They all seemed to believe that God in some mysterious
way had written the Bible and every word was true.
In the summer they had Sunday school
  at the schoolhouse.
Mrs. Stewart would play the organ.
She was huge and fat, and her buttocks
hung over the organ stool.  I worried it wouldn't
  hold her.
Sometimes when she had to nurse Baby Mary,

modestly covering up her large breast with a napkin,
Mrs. Schye would play the organ,
but the hymns had to be in flats, she couldn't
        play sharps.
Sometimes Wilma White played the organ.
She could only play by ear if she had heard the song
        before.
When her stepfather got her pregnant at fifteen,
she vanished and came no more.
The ladies took turns teaching Sunday school classes.
It was to be sure we knew all the stories.
One Sunday Mrs. Stewart was teaching the Ten Commandments.
When she came to the one about adultery,
I asked her what adultery was
(because I had looked it up in the dictionary).
She hemmed and hawed and said, "It is
taking something you shouldn't have."
I said, "When I steal cookies from the cookie jar,
am I committing adultery?"
        She didn't answer.
One time she was talking about marriage and children.
I asked her if Jesus had married
would his children have been little Gods?
        She didn't answer.
The Sunday school continued for years,
and the Ladies' Aid built up a little account.
Gradually the homesteaders failed and moved away.
Mrs. Schye was the last one left.
She had taken her mother's inheritance
and built a fine house on a high hill.
She took the money the Ladies' Aid had collected
and built a woven wire fence
        around the little cemetery
where some of the Ladies' Aid Society are now buried.

The ladies would get Preacher William
once a month to preach.
He was a sweet, gentle man, but when
        he preached,
he pounded the table and shouted
as though God were a horrible being
full of fire and brimstone
and we were doomed to hell if we didn't believe him
        and the Bible.
One day he bought a Ford Model T
and took everyone for a ride
with many children hanging on the running board.
It took him an hour to take everyone
        one mile.
Mrs. Baker would not take a ride
and fumed at her husband
for having taken a ride
in such a dangerous contraption
when he had six children at home.

*August 1988*

# The Day They Turned the Red Light Out

In this Montana barren land,
the principal products were sheep and cattle,
and as our town was on the Milwaukee Railroad,
the drovers and sheepherders brought their animals in
and the men went first to the Green Gable Hotel
     for a hot bath, then to the barber shop
where haircuts were fifty cents and a shave twenty-five
     cents.
Then, clean and liquored up, they went to the whorehouse
where for two dollars they could have a woman,
which they had not seen for many months,
although they said that some sheepherders used a
     docile ewe
to get rid of their pent-up sperm.
The ladies of the church became very angry.
They viewed sex as an ugly thing.
They often died in childbirth and there was no medicine
     to ease their pain at birthing.
They knew when they were frigid that their husbands
     went to a place of pleasure.
     The ladies worked all night but
     every afternoon they would dress up
     and parade the town.
They had great hats with ostrich plumes and flowers
     made in Mrs. Ryan's millinery shop
and gaudy silk dresses from the Erling Burt store.
They carried large lace parasols
and they would parade past the many saloons.
     The women of the Ladies' Aid Society
would pass them by with an angry sniff,
but when they passed a customer they would not
     give any sign of recognition.
One of the women kept her young daughter
with her in one of the small houses of the district,
and one night a kerosene lamp overturned, the house

burnt, and the child died.
The Ladies' Aid rose up in arms and
belabored the city fathers and the sheriff
and he sent many men to run the ladies out of town.
They had been friends and customers of the ladies
and they escorted them with all their baggage
and they left on the afternoon train
     and virtue returned to Ismay.
Shortly afterwards Prohibition came.
The last night there was shouting, shooting, and fighting.
     We cowered in our beds with an unknown fear.
The next morning the town was quiet.
The ladies of the night moved to the county seat
     where they maintained their business
     by sharing the profits with the politicians.
Speakeasys opened in many places,
and the isolated ranchers started making
     moonshine in hidden valleys.
In the drugstore we sold many products
     that were largely alcohol.
Lydia Pinkham's Vegetable Compound, which was
     made for women with female problems,
we sold by the case to sheepherders.
The town, like a bright green tree,
     started to slowly die,
dropping its leaves and branches one by one.
     People and businesses left, and
today just the church, Masonic temple, and post office
     remain.
The trains run only occasionally.
The ranchers send their animals out by truck.
The cure was successful, but the patient died!

*August 1988*

Main Street – Ismay, Montana.

Ismay sprang up overnight. As the Chicago, Milwaukee, St. Paul and Pacific Railroad moved its tracks westward, it established a town about every seven miles. Ismay was in an ideal location—the center of the sheep and cattle industry. Artesian water came to the surface when a well was dug. The O'Fallon River flowed nearby. Ismay was known as the little Chicago of the West. Many businesses flourished: two banks, two lumber yards, three hotels, four grocery stores, a drugstore, a general store, many saloons, a doctor, lawyer, and dentist. Also, the town boasted a fine school, running through four years of high school, three restaurants, several boarding houses, a telephone exchange, and an electric light plant, fully incorporated. It had a chamber of commerce. When the homesteaders arrived, they took up the land formerly used by large ranches. With the drought and dustbowl, the homesteaders moved away. The railroad stopped running. Then the Yellowstone Trail, a coast-to-coast highway, moved seven miles away and Ismay soon died. Today it has a post office, a Masonic temple, and a church. The houses were moved to other towns. Even though there is electricity and gas in all the vacant streets, only the cement sidewalks remain as they once were, when Ismay was a vibrant and happy town.

# Bracketts Butte

There is a high hill in eastern Montana
that can be seen in every direction.
It is a large volcanic extrusion
       filled with rocky boulders
       and rattlesnakes.
I never climbed it for fear of them.
Mr. Brackett was a buffalo hunter
       and made his camp near its foot.
He made a fortune by selling their hides.
And when he had made a small fortune,
he built a hotel in the emerging town of Ismay.
He kept one room filled with hides and hair
which we would use in our home talent plays.
       He had three daughters.
The oldest had a real literary brain;
she was an editor of a famous magazine.
She would come home to visit her parents
and me in the drugstore, where we had the
       first radio in town.
She introduced me to the joys of good music
       and read me beautiful literature.
She was homely and lonely in spite of her good position.
       She decided to have a baby.
She selected the handsomest man in town
although he was married.  She seduced him.
She said the baby was to have her brain and his looks.
       Strangely enough, it worked,
and her son became a powerful leader.
The second daughter, too, was homely.
       She graduated from college.
Through her father's influence she got a job
       teaching in the local high school.
She never seemed to bathe as there was no plumbing
       in the hotel.

She would walk the aisle of the study hall,
her satin petticoats rustling, but leaving behind
        an odor like month-old fish.
One night a handsome stranger came and stayed
        at the hotel.
In a few week's time he married her,
and after a short honeymoon
        in a fit of violent anger,
he shot her and splattered her blood all over
        the hotel office.
        He then shot himself.
The townspeople in anger wrapped his body in a
        blanket
and buried his body outside the cemetery,
but the sheriff made them dig it up and put it
        in a casket.
He was an escaped convict fleeing from the law.
The third daughter was very pretty.
She married a fine young rancher
        and raised many children.
Bracketts Butte still stands, a silent hill
seen from hundreds of miles.


*July 1988*

The Osters came to Ismay from the Ukraine. They spoke German, but we called them "Roosians." One night, George Oster heard a noise in the barn. He went out and someone shot him with a shotgun in the stomach, tied a rope to his leg, and dragged him through the sagebrush. The men of the community assembled and pursued the killer, but they didn't catch him. Destitute, the Widow Oster moved to Plevna, where there was a large German colony. She took in washing and somehow managed to keep her little family together. It was later revealed that the murderer was a member of a prominent family. He died before he could be prosecuted.

# The Last Great Cattle Ranch

Jim Boden discovered the area when he
brought great herds from Texas to fatten on
        the great Montana plains.
Most of the grounds of eastern Montana
had been given to the Crow Indians for a reservation,
but the politicians nibbled away at it so there
        was little left.
Jim returned to Texas, gathered a herd,
and returned to start a ranch.
With hired hands he built a ranch house
and a number of bunkhouses for the cowboys.
From the Pine Hills he gathered logs and
roofed them with the red iron oxide that he found.
Mr. Brackett had killed off all the buffalo
and left their bodies stinking on the plains.
The land surveyor came along and Jim found he was
        in the wrong spot
and so he took the buildings down and moved
        them to a spot he could own.
Jim was part Indian and he married a woman
        like him.
        The ranch prospered.
The homesteaders gradually fenced up the land,
but there was much land left in the
open school section and the public land.
All went well until the terrible snow storm of 1916.
The snow became so deep that all the fences were
        covered
and all of the roads became impassable.
Huge herds of cattle and sheep lay buried in the snow.
That spring as we walked to visit our grandmother,
we had to hold our noses because of the
        stench that fouled the air.
One cow lay dead with her calf half extended
as she had been smothered while birthing it.

This storm was the end of Jim's cattle venture.
At this time a movement was sweeping the northwest,
                    called the Non-Partisan League.
It was a socialistic movement
where people should share in all businesses.
Each community was to own its own banks,
                    flour mills, and creamery.
The First National Bank was already in existence
and had a fine brick building with offices upstairs.
A First State Bank was formed; it too had a good
                    brick building.
It ran just a short time and the cashier went to
                    prison.
While the money was collected for a flour mill,
                    it was never built.
The creamery was built, but as they had no
                    refrigeration,
the product was poor and the creamery closed.
Jim lost much money and some accused him of cheating.
He bought a grain separator,
and when he was threshing on the McKee's place,
                    it burned.
Jim had three children.
From the time his son Floyd could ride a horse,
he rode with the cowboys.
At fifteen he was tall, dark, and handsome.
                    I was in the second grade
                    and we would all wait and watch
                    to see him come to school.
When he arrived at the gate in the barbed wire fence,
he would make his horse jump the barbed wire.
He was unmindful that, if the horse slipped or couldn't
                    make it,
they both might have been hurt in the barbed wire.
His father built a small barn on the school ground

and would only let his son stable their horses there.
This caused a great deal of angry comment.
His daughter, Joyce, was a spoilt child.
She did not want to do her work in school,
and Mrs. Shaw gave her poor grades.
Her angry mother came to school
and pummeled the teacher.
There was screaming and yelling and pulling of hair
while the frightened children watched.
Joyce was given everything she wanted,
and when she graduated from the eighth grade,
she wore a low-cut evening dress of velvet.
When she went to high school,
her father bought her a Model T.
She would drive dizzily down the dirt road,
honking at everyone to get out of the way.
She flirted much and she was knocked up
by the leading handsome bronco rider.
Her mother gave her an abortion with a hatpin
                    and poor Joyce died.
They had kept her body too long,
and she was buried by lantern light
in the North Cottonwood cemetery.
Shortly after Joyce's death,
                    Jim languished and died.
It was said that at the funeral
a little Russian homesteader
was heard to say, "Jim won't cheat anyone any more."
That night the Russian, a father of four children,
heard a noise coming from the barn.
He went to investigate
and someone shot him in the stomach
and dragged his body through the sagebrush.
Poor frightened Mrs. Oster rang the alarm line

on the party telephone,
and all the local farmers gathered by lantern light
until in the morning they could follow the tracks
                    of the horse of the murderer.
They found Jim's boy, Floyd, trimming his horse's hoof.
He was arrested, but they dropped the charges.
Luckily so, because another close rancher,
                    who had been in prison,
was found to have done the crime.
The bank foreclosed on the ranch.
Mrs. Boden went to work as a housekeeper in another
                    ranch.
One night she went for a walk and did not return.
In the spring when the snows had melted,
they found her old worn body.
She had climbed the highest hill
where she could look down on the ranch
that had once been her busy home.
She died and the winter freezes and snows
                    preserved her body.
She was buried in the North Cottonwood cemetery
alongside her greatly beloved daughter, Joyce.


*August 1988*

# The Schoolteacher

The first sound we heard was the
loud ringing of the alarm clock
on that cold December morning
and then the sound of my father
cranking down the noisy grates
to replenish the last embers of the coal fire
that had kept the house from freezing.
The next sound was the sound of the coffee grinder
followed  by the rich smell of coffee.
Father bundled up and went to milk the cows.
It was time to get up.
It had snowed during the night,
and we had to avoid the patches of snow
that had sifted through the cracks
                of our attic bedroom.
We hurried down the stairs to the center stove
and dressed, turning our little behinds
                to the glowing fire.
There was a breakfast of oatmeal that
had been soaked during the night before cooking
and pancakes with thick corn syrup.
John, the eldest, went out to harness
and hitch old Frank and Roanie to the buggy.
Mother put up the lunches and a pot of bean soup
to feed the many children of her country school.
There had been a chance for a crop that year,
but one spring morning we awoke
to find the cutworm, during the night,
had cut off all the crops at the roots
and the crop lay wilted on the ground.
The only resource left was the clever brain
                of my mother.
She took an examination that qualified her
and secured a contract to teach the local school
of sixteen students; four of them

were her sons, John, Charles, Richard, and Edgar.
At seven we climbed into the buggy
to make the long, cold ride to the lonesome
North Cottonwood School, two miles away.
After a slow trip we arrived.
John unharnessed the horses.
I lit the huge fire in the stove in the center of the room.
Richard and Edgar washed the blackboards and
                    dusted the erasers.
I corrected papers and mother prepared the lessons
for the eight grades following the state course of study.
At nine she rang the school bell
and the children, standing in line, marched in
and hung their coats in the cloakroom
which also contained the water bucket.
There was no longer a common tin dipper
used by all the students and the previous teacher,
but a row of neat china cups with our names attached.
We opened the day with a salute to the flag,
a brief prayer, and a reading from
                    some great book.
That morning it was *Gulliver's Travels* and she quit
                    reading
when the Lilliputians had Gulliver strapped to the ground.
She would continue reading after the noon recess,
when all would share the rich bean soup she heated
                    on the heater.
We had been reading the story of the fall of Troy,
and Mother had a sand table in the corner
where we made a model of the town of Troy.
John and Elmer Schye added a model of the wooden horse.
If one of the little children couldn't read,
an older child was assigned to sit with them
and point out the words they missed.
Our poem to be memorized that day was "Daffodils":

"I wandered lonely as a cloud
That floats on high o'er dale or hill
And all at once I saw
A host of golden daffodils..."
I had never seen a daffodil, but
I knew what the author meant
because I had felt as lonely as a cloud
and seen a field of beauty, not of daffodils,
> but of spring crocuses
> that followed the winter snow drifts.

We had not known how to address our mother
and decided we would call her "Mam."
John, age fifteen, was the disciplinarian of the school.
If any boy acted out of line, he knew
he would have to fight a Beardsley boy of equal size.
Mother never knew what went on at recess.
She couldn't understand why sometimes we would come in
after recess with bloody noses.
I fear I suffered most
because Elmer Schye was older, bigger, and stronger,
but I never lost, although I sometimes wanted to turn and run.
I was helping my mother because the other boys
> had been naughty.

That day she asked us the height of the flagpole
> outside in the playground.

When we could not answer, she taught us triangulation,
> using the shadow as the side of a triangle.

When we read about South America,
we made a map of salt and flour and
on it we would fasten the principal products.

In hygiene she had us draw a map of our water
> supply, either springs or wells,

and place all points of contagion, barns, outhouses,
> or manure piles.

She had us figure out what the local
                store got for an ounce of cornflakes
and what our fathers got for corn—it was three cents.
Each class took turns in reading
by coming up to the long recitation bench
to assure her that they knew everything in their textbooks.
The day closed with a spelling bee.
We were always proud of the day we could go home
                and say we were the best spellers.
The day ended, we would make the long trip home,
the buggy wheels creaking in the snow.
Mother would bake the bread for the next day.
                I would do the dishes.
John would feed the pigs and chickens
and put the horses out to pasture.
Richard and Edgar would turn the wooden churn
to make the fresh yellow butter.
After supper of snow potatoes and meat
and vegetables, canned the previous summer,
we would study our lessons and close
                with a game of cards.
And so to bed.  She would promise us that,
if we would go to bed quietly, she would play us two
records:  A Sousa march or a Caruso song
on the 1910 squeaky but beautiful phonograph.
Spring came again, but this time
John, 15, Elmer, 14, and I, 12, had to take
a state examination
of what we had learned in school.
Arithmetic, geography, language, history, agriculture.
We all passed, the only ones
in a county of seventy rural schools.
John, who learned all the good lessons in life
and started with my father's debts against
the small homestead,  became the grand old patriarch

and left behind a ranch of forty-eight square miles,
eight successful children, and fifty descendants.
Elmer was to become the mayor of his town.
I was to travel far, attend many colleges, and receive
many awards.
I think much of it happened in that one-room school
                with my beautiful mother
beaming at us proudly behind the teacher's desk.


*July 1988*

This was the second house my parents built on the homestead; the first was a
tarpaper shack. This house was built on a high hill so that we could see as far
as the eye, but we had to haul the household water a mile and a half. My
folks borrowed $1,000 at 10 percent interest to build the house, and they lived
there for nineteen years. My brother John finally paid off the mortgage. He
later sold the house for $500, and it was torn down and rebuilt in Miles City,
seventy miles away.

# The Wish Book

It was in the late summer the winter wish book came
filled with all the dreams our little hearts
           could wish for.
Last year's wish book was sent to the outhouse,
where all the soft grey sheets of harness and farm
           tools were first to go,
leaving behind the shiny colored sheets
           of fancy women's clothing.

Oh, the wonders of the new wish book.
We selected all the things our hearts
           would have for those we loved.
In our hearts we knew it could not be.
The hired man worked for one dollar a day.
The hired girl for room and board.
Sometimes all the money in the house
came from selling eggs at five cents a dozen
or a quart of cream for twenty cents.

The grand glory of our dreams was
           stronger than reality.
A shiny kitchen stove all black and glistening
           with a glow of nickel
for our mother with a cost of twenty-four dollars.
A sable fur-lined greatcoat for fifty dollars
           for our father.

A warm cloth coat with caracul collar
           for eighteen dollars for sister Elizabeth.
For brother John a hunter's watch with
           an antlered stag upon its case.
Just books for me,
I did not desire any other thing

for with books
I saw the world.

For brother Dick a wind-up train and track
                    for just two dollars.
For little Edgar a little trike with a
glistening bell for just four dollars.

One late Christmas evening our father
                    climbed to the roof of the high house
And, risking life and limb, stomped on the roof,
shouting "Ho ho ho!" and ringing sleigh bells.

We cuddled in our feather beds
and dreamed of all the happy things
the Christmas morning would bring.
And with excitement the early Christmas morn
found us screaming down the stairs
from our bed in the loft,
where the snow sifted in during the night,
to find our gifts for each upon his chair.
                    All the little gifts
our parents and our family could afford.
They were just as great as the
beautiful things in the wish book.

# The Fishing Trip

We had all dreamed of going fishing.
The nearest water was fifteen miles away
                on the O'Fallon River.
John and I rose early.
John saddled the horses and I put up
a lunch to carry in the saddle bags.
We gathered at the North Cottonwood School
and started down North Cottonwood Creek.
Dry now, because it only had water
when the snows of winter melted.
There were ten of us.  Clayton Carey was
the oldest and I was the youngest,
and poor little Shorty Vroman, whom God
                had not completely finished.
We rode past the ruins of my grandmother's homestead.
We passed old maid Johnson's deserted house
with dirty lace curtains still hanging from the windows
and a smelly privy leaning crazily over a smelly hole.
When the homestead failed, she had departed for
                parts unknown.
We arrived at O'Fallon River,  and in a clump of
                dusty willows,
we set up our lunch on our sweaty saddle blankets.
We tried to fish, but the stale yellow, alkaline water
yielded nothing but frogs.
We ate our lunch and drank water from a hot canteen.
We turned to talk about sex and babies.
The ranches we came from all depended
upon the young of their animals,
horses, cows, pigs, chickens, turkeys, and ducks.
We had watched them in action.
Finally we talked about how people made babies,
the girls that would, and the girls that wouldn't,
and the woman of the little town who, for two dollars, would.

They decided each would show his cock.
Clayton Carey was the oldest and the first.
It seemed he had had the most women.
He was followed by his brother, Victor,
                    the one with the crippled foot.
Finally it came to Shorty Vroman.
                    He didn't want to do it.
They took him down and held his arms and legs,
and each took turns spitting on his cock.
                    Shorty started to cry and sob.
                    They let him go.
I had sat cowering under a nearby tree.
After Shorty's tears they stopped picking on him.
                    I was saved by his tears.
                    We rode the long miles home.
I can still see and hear Shorty's sad weeping.


*August 1988*

# Savior of Souls

He came to town with large ads in the *Ismay Journal*.
There was little entertainment in this lonely town.
He was tall and walked in silent loneliness
and would not speak after his stormy sermon,
except at the conclusion of the service
when, if the take was good, he would weakly smile.
It seemed that everything we did was wrong.
Dancing after midnight at the Saturday night dances,
playing cards at the card parties, which were the means
to break the monotony of the country life.
Everything we did seemed wrong.
He made us feel guilty.
Only Jesus could save us from the
              loneliness of our souls.
He had a beautiful daughter with a beautiful voice.
              Each night he made her sing.
She later told me she hated it all;
              she wanted to be with young people.
The town turned out, there was little else to do.
Each night his beautiful daughter sang,
              "Just as I am."
People would come forward and kneel at the altar rail,
and he would come forward and put his cold hands
on their heads if they accepted Jesus Christ as their
              personal Savior.
It seemed everyone came forward.
Since everyone did it, I thought I would try.
Nothing happened—but I looked up
and saw the face of his beautiful daughter.
I had heard soft murmurs about the nature of God.
I did not meet a man called Jesus.
I saw her sweet face and loved her.
The man left town, taking my first love with him.
He didn't pay his grocery bill he had charged
              at the Earling Burt Store.

# The Sunday School Teacher

She had married young and lived sixty
                    miles from town.
          She had no close neighbors.
Her husband contracted the 1917 flu bug
and she tended him, listening to his wracking cough,
          putting cool cloths on his head,
          and holding his hot, dry hand.
But he died in one last gasp for breath.
She saddled up a horse and rode five miles
to get help from the nearest neighbor
to help her bury her dead husband in a lonely grave.
She came to town, lived with her parents, and
          worked in the largest store.
She taught Sunday school and made the colorful myths
          of the Old Testament come alive.
At Easter and Christmas she led a children's choir.
How proud we were when she proudly directed us.
In those days a widow was open game
          for any insincere philandering man.
Deprived of the strong arms of a loving man,
she selected one of the handsomest men in town.
He was tall, muscular, with wavy grey hair,
but he was married to the ugliest woman in town.
She would stride through town with her chin protruding
          like the prow of a battleship.
One night our teacher had a meeting with him
          on the couch in his locked office.
          He forgot his wife had a key.

She walked in and, seeing them naked on the couch,
grabbed all their clothes and went down the street,
screaming at passersby, "See what they are doing in
                                    there!"
The couple had to leave wrapped in old newspapers.
We did not think the less of her.
                    Next Sunday she was in church
                    leading her happy class.
We still loved her—children do not condemn.
She had taught us the story of Mary Magdalene very well,
that complete love is both forgiveness and acceptance.


*July 1988*

Little Joanne Beardsley Perkins, sitting on the porch of J. M. Baker's house with the North Cottonwood School in the background (where her mother, Ella Teats Beardsley, her aunt, Elizabeth Beardsley Bartels, and her grandmother, Alice Broman Beardsley, taught school).

She was the first-born of John Henry Beardsley and the oldest of eight children. She inherited great mental genes, as brothers of her father and mother won Rhodes scholarships and graduated from Oxford, England.

After helping take care of her brothers and sisters and her father's huge ranch, she became a teacher—first teaching girls' physical education, then disadvantaged students in Custer County High School, Miles City, Montana.

When the people of the community vanished, the schoolhouse was hauled away to become a granary at a distant farmer's ranch. The house was likewise hauled away.

# Transition

A hymn to the joy of living
And an affirmation of life.

Whenever you walk those treasured
       happy paths
That we have walked before
And do not meet me,
Be not afraid for I am there.

The gentle breeze that cools your face
Is the hand you held so tenderly before.

The sunset in the gleaming azure sky
Is the joy we felt so tenderly before.

Take the hand of some poor frightened child.
This I have been
And in him I shall also be.

And if you would feed me
At your sumptuous board,
Heed to the lonesome stranger knocking
At  your door;
For I have lost and lonely been.

Talk to him and tell him
Of the great generic love
We both have felt and known so well.

When the last breath has left this
Frail and fragile form,
If any human parts are usable
Give them to anyone in need of them.

And what is left send to the brilliant
Sunlike flame that all these parts
May be released to live in glowing glory,
To live in growing flowering plants,
And in the winds that sweep
This great loved earth.

Do not meet to mourn my passing
For we have met in joy and laughter;
And we should part the same.

Sing and dance, let laughter ring
For soon again we shall meet in
Joyousness we have not known before.

Do not pause before a silent stone to weep
        or by some mouldering grave
        or yet a dusty sepulchre,
For can you think that I, who loved the earth so well
Would linger in such an awful place.

Treasure the little things I leave behind.
They were but a loan to me
From those who loved me well.

Men struggle to make remembrance
An eternal thing
And if some small figment is left behind
By which I shall be remembered
I shall be content.

The gentle carpenter who reached divine perfection
Wrote but one single sentence that we know,

"That he who has committed error cannot
			condemn those who err."

The burly thinker of the Athens' square
Was condemned to die
Because he said, "The unexamined life is not
			worth living."
And they were afraid when they searched
The deeds that they had done.

And the healing doctor in the jungle grove
And the gentle saint who loved
		all living things,
Each left behind three lifelong words,
	"Reverence for life."
And if some thought I could leave behind
			would be but two
That in my short time,
			"I loved."


*January 1980*

# The Candles of My Mind

I was born a stranger in a strange and arid land
A land where lonesome distance stretched
                endless to the sky.
And yet I knew that I was meant to be and
Being meant to be proved there that I should be.

I hungered for clear running streams
And trees whose cooling shade would
                give me rest and comfort
Or views of rugged mountains piercing
A bright and cloud-filled sky.

Sometimes in the hidden silences of the night
I could hear the rumblings of the distant sea
When I looked upon the dry and arid plain
                I only saw the rolling tumble weed
And the hungry cattle backward
To the harsh and driving wind.

I do not know that I was placed there
To receive the love that was to be
                the nurture and my strength
I think it was my mother who lit
                the candles of my mind
And made it that I might within
Store the magic that is knowledge.

I have wandered far and often when I
                turn some sudden corner
I know it is a place where I have been
Before in this transient life.

Sometimes when I hear a voice or see a face
Soft murmurings from out the distant past
              stir in my mind to tell me
What is now has also been in then.

I had no final or ultimate knowledge to give
              them, for none there was nor is
All learned subjects of my youth
              have been disclaimed
And all the so-called facts we now acclaim
Will be as "witchcraft" when the span of years
              has run their course.

Young I learned that it is greater
              to feel in harmony with all things
And what we think we know is often false
Therefore what we feel is all
              there is to now
And all of what we know
Will crumble in the dust.

I have had a guide that led me
              on my often stumbling path
I could not see his face, but
My little grandson whose gentle mind
              untrammeled could cast out time
And see what was in then and what is soon to be,
              he defined the unknown face to me
And I was comforted to know my guide.

Sometimes within a problemed space
My heart was fearful and I did not
                know the way to go.
The gentle guide told me where and what
                was to be and twice he
Led me from the cold hands of death.

In June I sat upon the ancient squared stone seats
                that once was the theatre at Delphi
Where bright young actors portrayed the
                state that is the life of Man
And suddenly instead of aging crumbled stone
White clean and golden temples appeared.

And through the distant mountain
Pass great armies of power-driven men
                came to clamor at the ancient gaseous
Vent where they thought the knowledge
Of their destiny would appear.

In the playing field behind me
Strong young men with gleaming muscled bodies
                showed forth their naked strength
And received a crown of humble laurel
For their praises.

As I sat there, a greyed and learned man said
You were a teacher in the long ago
                And I can see your face as you were then
In my heart I was at peace
For I knew that this was true.

In a strange way the path has led me
To a place I once called home
              some strange and loving force
Had caused to change my mind from flickering candle
That can pierce the death of nothingness.

To a bright universe of light where
Myriad stars go sweeping in vast
              expanding space in the
Great joy that is creation
For we are in creation a burning part of it.

And sometimes the only purpose of it all
Is there are kindly students who say
              that I have taught them all they knew
This is not so for I have not
Truth but that I am.

They must be their only teachers to themselves
Feeding on the growth of others
              to make a sometime truth consistent
With their own in their search for truth
Find out why it is we are to be and am and were.

For they all are one and I am one with them.

*1980*

# About the Author

Dr. Charles P. Beardsley has had a varied career. He has attended nine colleges and taught in every type of school from a rural school (with all grades) to graduate school. He has taught in two universities, four high schools, and one college and has received several awards for excellence in teaching.

Dr. Beardsley's biography is included in the *World Wide Book of Intellectuals*, Seventh Edition, published in England. He was given the Award of Merit from Eastern Montana College and nominated that school's outstanding graduate. He received the Humanitarian Award from Arizona State University in Tempe, and in 1988 he was given the Doctor of Humanities Award from World University. He was named deputy director of the International Biographical Society for the United States and given a medal and plaque and was appointed principal speaker at the International Biographical Congress in Madrid, Spain. As a musical conductor he has received national recognition and been awarded a plaque from the state of California for his work in music and art.

He has been the head of many organizations in the business world and has been recognized nationally and internationally. He has been awarded six plaques from the California Real Estate Board for being the director of several boards. He was chairman of the Resort Properties Commission, president of Tahoe Sierra Board of Realtors, and vice president of the state realtors' organization.

He started writing when he was twelve years old, and he won a $5 prize for the best story in Custer County, Montana. He has written many historical articles, plays, poems, and the librettos for two operettas. His poem "Transition" won third prize in an international poetry contest in Rome, Italy, and has appeared in many publications.

Dr. Beardsley lives in Sonoma, California, after retiring from Merritt College in Oakland, California, and the business world. He spent seven years restoring General Vallejo's sawmill near Sonoma, the site of the first water wheel, the first sawmill and flour mill, and one of the first, and largest, wineries. He has been president of the Sonoma Valley Historical Society, chairman of the Cultural and Fine Arts Commission, and a director of the Sonoma State Parks Board.

Dr. Beardsley spends his time maintaining his private museum of Indian and historical artifacts, ten antique keyboard instruments, and art collection.

He wrote this book for his daughter, Elsbeth St. Ives, and four grandchildren and his many spiritual children, so that they may know from whence he came. He did not want this brief but important period to pass unrecorded.